Popcorn Miracles®

Little Reminders of God's Nearness

Bob and Gail Kaku

 MAJESTYHOUSE®

Published by Majesty House®
www.majestyhouse.com
Cover design by Kristina Szeto

Library of Congress Control Number: 2008900903
ISBN-10 0-9799903-0-0
ISBN-13 978-0-9799903-0-4
Printed in the United States of America

*This book is dedicated to those who
want popcorn miracles in their lives.*

FOREWORD

Bob and Gail tell delightful tales of experiencing extraordinary interventions in the midst of the ordinary sort of life you and I live. Each story gives simple testimony to an astounding aspect of the relationship God offers each of us; you might call it *the nearness of God.*

Contrary to what you might imagine, He is not a God who remains far off, aloof from our daily quandaries; rather, time and again, He reveals Himself as a *very present help-giver*, a sustainer and guide, an encouraging, watchful, safe counselor. These accounts provide a remarkable vantage point from which anyone can glimpse the incredible *immediacy of God*—right here and now.

Those of us who have walked with God on a daily path like theirs will find the stories delightfully familiar and can often guess how the Lord is going to intervene. If you are still considering what your life will be like if you offer it to Jesus, these accounts will give you a fast-forward viewing.

Popcorn Miracles has a tender intimacy that lingers from page to page, as though written on paper scented with closeness and affection. In part, that tenderness comes from the welcomed simplicity of what they relate—testimonies stripped of all theological jargon and hype. Mostly, however, the intimacy that permeates all of what they tell us has its source in the One about whom they write. His Name is Jesus, and He wants to walk with you, too, all the days of your life.

Daniel A. Brown, PhD.
Aptos, California

CONTENTS

CONTENTS

ACKNOWLEDGMENTS

Popcorn Miracles would not have been possible without the help of many people who contributed to its creation. Our deepest gratitude goes to the leaders of our two critique groups, Ethel Herr and Rick Hinz, and group participants: Stephanie Shoquist, Sandra Gutknecht, Adam McDonald, Pamela Chang JD, Robert Schaetzle, Allan Cobb, Robert Fitch, Bill and Betty Lien, and Kay Gutknecht.

We want to acknowledge others who sacrificially spent countless hours reading, editing, and providing comments on the entire manuscript, some more than once: Patsy Oda, Nana Nishida, Mabel Okamura, Christine Sato, Carolyn Shimabukuro, Cyril Nishimoto JD, Pauline Nishida, Coleen Nakamura, and Yuki Suminaga.

Our heartfelt thanks go to those who provided inputs to stories: Paul Tabe, Mark Baba, George Toyama, Ross Fujino, Wendy Farnsworth, Dee Melconian, Chrislee Gedeon, Ben Asaka, Kelly Lee, Trina Lee, Terry Lee, Sarah Gabot, Brian Gabot, Dr. Gordon Brody, and Dr. Bob Yonemoto.

We're humbled by all those who prayed, provided comments, and encouragement: Jonathan and Marlene Jones, Charles Dancak, Jan Coleman, Irene Takamine, Dave Shoquist, Dick Bernal, Sandra Dunn, Bob Nakahara, Pati Toy, Mits Tomita, Roland Hazama, Rob Yonemoto, Stan Date, Janet Nagatoshi, and Jacqueline Farnsworth, PhD.

We thank Tom Neven, Karen O'Connor, Brandilyn Collins, Christine Tangvald, Randy Ingermanson, PhD, and all those who provided wise counsel at the Mount Hermon writers conferences, and Chicken Soup for the Soul conference. We extend hearty thanks to James Scott Bell JD, Nick Harrison, and Lin Johnson who provided invaluable advice during the Northwest writers cruise.

We are most grateful to Daniel A. Brown, PhD, who wrote the Foreword and provided expert advice.

We thank our editors Erin Brown, Elaine Irao, and Skylar Burris for their tireless efforts editing the manuscript.

Our sincere appreciation goes to Kristina Szeto for all her hard work on the cover design.

We owe a debt of gratitude to Barry Adams for granting us permission to include the "Father's Love Letter."

Finally, we thank all those who have participated in the birthing of this book. Above all, we're grateful to our Lord Jesus Christ who guided us through every phase of the book's creation process.

INTRODUCTION

Popcorn Miracles are true, inspirational stories about extraordinary events in everyday life. These are little "popcorn-sized" reminders of the nearness of God and how He cares about every aspect of your life from the triumphs to the struggles, both large and small.

These stories recount miracles, answered prayers, healings, and provisions. You may laugh, cry, or remember some of your own similar experiences. They are intended to encourage you, build faith, and help you find God. Some stories are light and fun to read. Others are weighty, like the hard un-popped kernels found at the bottom of every popcorn box.

It was during a Bible study that Gail heard the small, inner voice of the Lord say, "Tell the people the great things I have done." This message kept recurring.

"Some day, we'll write a book about it," she thought.

The following verses spoke to our hearts and became the theme of our book:

> "Give thanks to the LORD, call on his name; make known among the nations what he has done, and proclaim that his name is exalted. Sing to the LORD, for he has done glorious things; let this be known to all the world" (Isaiah 12:4–5 NIV).

It's important to understand that God did all these things. It's *not* about us.

Initially, we had a difficult time coming up with a title, but after we sought the Lord, *Popcorn Miracles* "popped" into Bob's mind. We thought, "Yes, of course, 'popcorn'—small as in popcorn shrimp or popcorn chicken." When a kernel of corn pops, it explodes into a light, fluffy, and unique morsel.

We pray this book will show you how much God loves you and how real He is. He understands you in such intricate detail that He even knows the number of hairs on your head. It is His desire for you to have a dynamic and intimate relationship with Him.

Bon appétit!

~ Bob and Gail Kaku

Chapter 1   CALL HIM UP

God's love for us is great, immeasurable, and unconditional; it is deeper than the ocean, higher than the moon and stars, and larger than the universe. When we cry out to Him with all our hearts, He hears us. He wants to be involved in our lives.

ॐ ༘ ৶

The Key

*U*nder crystalline blue skies, my wife, Gail, and I basked in the tranquility of St. John, US Virgin Islands. The warm, azure waters washed our feet as we waded through the gentle waves. The unhurried pace and friendly banter with the locals were a welcomed respite from our hectic Californian lives.

We drank in the spectacular vistas of Cruz Bay and the Caribbean from the veranda of our rented condo perched atop a steep hill. The balmy onshore breeze and melodic cadence of steel drums wafted in, making our stress float away. What a relaxing spot! Everything was perfect until . . .

One evening, we strolled down to the swimming pool, the perfect vantage point to view the glistening harbor lights on one side and the shimmering moonlit sea on the other. Periodic boat horns droned in the distance. After we sauntered back to our unit, I fished through my belt pouch and pockets for the key, but I couldn't find it. All week I had used extreme caution putting the key back into my pouch. I peered through the kitchen window and saw the key sitting on the counter. "OH, NO! There's no night manager. How will we get in?"

"Something always happens on our vacations. I usually ask for a second key," Gail chided herself.

After collecting my thoughts, I grabbed a condo brochure from the display case outside the dark office. The manager's phone number was on it.

We drove down the steep road in our rental Jeep and pulled into a hotel. I called the manager and left a message telling her we were locked out and to call the hotel lobby.

I found her home address in the telephone book. While Gail waited in the lobby, I drove off to find the manager's house. The streets meandered in endless confusion. The same names seemed to identify different streets. On top of that, house numbers were either missing or hidden behind the tropical foliage. I asked several people for directions, but they were tourists. After an hour, I gave up and drove back to the hotel.

Gail prayed in the hotel lobby. "Jesus, please help us with this problem!" After praying she urged me to call the manager again. When I called, the answering machine beeped. Her eyes sank to the floor. "We can stay in the hotel tonight, but it's $175 on top of what we already paid."

"Maybe the manager shut off her phone for the evening. We can sleep in the Jeep. The seats fold down."

She scowled. "But I'm wearing my contact lenses, and I can't sleep with them."

I thumbed through the Yellow Pages to search for a locksmith. "This island doesn't have a locksmith? The only ones listed are clear across the sea channel in St. Thomas."

"You've got to be kidding." Gail prayed again and rebounded. "Nothing is too difficult for the Lord. Perhaps the manager is back at the condo. Why don't you drive over there while I wait by the phone?"

When I arrived at the condo complex, the parking lot was empty. *No sign of the manager here.* I was about to drive back to the hotel when something compelled me to get out of the Jeep and walk over to our condo. A woman in the adjacent unit was preparing dinner. I knocked on the door and her husband answered.

"I'm locked out," I said. "I called the office but kept getting the answering machine. Do you know how to contact the manager?"

"I don't know," he replied. "Let's see if my key will work. I don't think it will, but what the heck."

Is he kidding?

We strode down to my unit. He slid his key into the door lock and turned the knob. The door whooshed open. I stared bug-eyed with my mouth wide open. *Whoa! How can that be?* I exuberantly thanked the man and drove back to the hotel to pick up Gail.

"What?" she shrieked and burst into laughter. "I can't believe it. Thank You Jesus!"

After returning to the condo, I left another message for the manager, letting her know we got in.

"I wonder if any key would open any unit," Gail said. Just to test this possibility, we descended the stairs to try our key on an unoccupied unit. The key slid into the door lock, but it wouldn't turn. "Hmm—maybe we share a common key only with our neighbor?"

The following morning, the manager and the housekeeper scurried over. "How did you get in?" the manager asked.

After we explained everything, the housekeeper covered her mouth with her hand. "Ohh! I misplaced a master key."

Out of the ten condo units, the people in the unit adjacent to us just so happened to be in that night and just so happened to have that improbable key.

Then they cried out to the LORD in their trouble; He delivered them out of their distresses. (Psalm 107:6)

~ Bob Kaku

෨ 🕊 ෬

Like That's Really Going to Help

*M*y stomach churned as I looked down the steep, forbidding ski slope at June Mountain, a popular resort located on the eastern side of California's Sierra Nevada Mountains. I cried out to my friend Mark, "This run is too hard for me!"

Mark, a proficient skier, had zipped halfway down the intermediate-level run and was waiting for me to come down. "Try traversing it, Gail."

Maybe I projected myself as an expert skier. I hadn't told him I had skied only twice before.

I drove up to the ski resort with Mark. This was during my single days when I went skiing with a group of church friends. What a day! Everything went wrong from the get-go. I rented my skis and boots from a local shop, but they were out of poles. We went to the ski lodge to rent them and waited nearly an hour in seemingly endless checkout lines. The lengthy delay annoyed Mark as it cut into our ski time on this picture-perfect, blue-sky day.

Now, this! Gravity tugged at me as I leaned over the edge. When I saw there was no easy way down, I gingerly traversed the run. My heart thumped as I swerved into a half-moon turn, lost my balance, and plunged into the snow.

With the aid of the poles, I pushed myself upright.

Turning toward the fall line, I started down again, but soon I crossed my ski tips and took another spill.

Mark sidestepped up the hill to help me. When I stood to my feet, I noticed blurred vision out of my left eye. "Nnnoo! My contact lens fell out!"

We squatted down and searched for the contact lens with our gloved hands. The glistening white snow and contrasting shadows cast by the sunlight over the bumps and ruts made it difficult to spot the small piece of plastic. To make matters worse, snow kicked up by other skiers flew all around the area.

"I think the lens dropped near my left ski." I moved the ski away, but it wasn't there. We continued searching, but to no avail. "Can we pray about this?" I asked.

Mark rolled his eyes as if he was about to say, "Like that's really going to help."

I prayed aloud anyway. "Dear Jesus, we commit the contact lens to you. Please help us find it."

Immediately after praying, Mark fixed his gaze straight down near his ski. "I found the lens!" he said. He leaned over to pick it up and handed it to me with a dumbfounded smile.

He had to admit—God answered my prayer.

Ask, and it will be given to you; seek, and you will find; knock, and it will be opened to you. (Matthew 7:7)

~ Gail Kaku

❧ 🕊 ☙

Jesus Elsker Deg

*M*y travel companion, Ginny, and I were having the time of our lives, backpacking throughout Western Europe and meeting all sorts of interesting people from around the world.

When we arrived in Oslo, Norway, I marveled at the sight of so many blond and blue-eyed Scandinavians. We strolled past charming cafés and inviting shops in the Land of the Midnight Sun where daylight stretched well into the summer nights.

A friendly Norwegian couple at the rail station lugged our heavy backpacks, bought us ice cream, and kissed us good-bye as we departed for our next destination. From Oslo, we traveled along the southwestern coast to Stavanger.

My American friend John and his Norwegian wife, Lindis, accommodated us at their home for three days. They took us sightseeing all over this charming port city—a blend of an old town and a modern city, set against a backdrop of towering mountains that plunge dramatically into deep fjords.

On a pastel, blue-sky day, they took Ginny and me to a picnic at a nearby park. While we were eating lunch, a loud, cantankerous drunk staggered toward us. "Arrgh!" he growled, kicking tin cans into the air. With a beet-red face and clenched fists, he appeared ready to take a swing at anyone who looked at him. My heart quickened.

The drunken man drew closer to us, and his shouts grew louder and louder. John walked over to him and looked him straight in the eyes with compassion.

My knees jellied. *What's John doing?*

John mumbled something to him. Almost instantly, the man's belligerent expression softened. He waddled backward, humbly nodded to each person and shuffled away.

"Lindis, what did John say?"

"He said, '*Jesus elsker deg,* which means Jesus loves you in Norwegian.' "

The power of those three little words astounded me.

Therefore God also has highly exalted Him and given Him the name which is above every name, that at the name of Jesus every knee should bow (Philippians 2:9–10 NKJV)

~ Gail Kaku

∝ 🕊 ∝

Whiteout

That's not possible. I looked at the ticket agent in disbelief. "You mean I'm not in Redmond?"

"I'm afraid not. You're in Medford," he answered.

My Seattle friends planned a weekend ski trip to Mount Bachelor and were waiting for me at the Redmond, Oregon airport. I had been blind-sided by an airline schedule change that added an extra stopover in Medford, Oregon.

"There aren't any more flights to Redmond tonight," the ticket agent said. "The earliest flight isn't until tomorrow morning. It'll reroute you back to San Francisco, connect through Portland, and then to Redmond."

My heart sank. "Is there a bus I can take?"

"There aren't any buses into Redmond."

These were the days before cell phones. The ticket agent called the Redmond airport, had my friend paged, and handed me the phone.

"You're not going to believe what happened . . ."

After considering my options, I decided to rent a car and drive about 170 miles to Sunriver Lodge where my friends were staying. Several minutes after I pulled out of the car rental lot, snow began to fall. *I don't believe it. Lord, please don't let it snow.* Soon the snow flurries became heavier. *I'm going to need tire chains!*

I pulled into a convenience store to purchase snow chains. "You never installed tire chains before?" the store manager asked with concern.

"No."

He demonstrated how to put on chains, gave me a crash course on driving through snow and ice, and provided directions to Sunriver.

Within minutes, I found myself driving in a blizzard on a treacherous mountain highway. Occasionally, a truck or car whizzed by and illuminated the pitch-dark road. Since I had good traction, I decided not to use chains. The intermittent fog and heavy snow on the windshield obscured my vision. Since I couldn't pick up any radio signals, I only heard the syncopated wiper blades scraping furiously. At times the road seemed to disappear. I ran the defroster full blast and trembled with fear.

"Lord, please help me through this snowstorm! If I don't make it, please forgive me for all those times I hurt You and for my multitude of sins . . ."

As I was driving, I sensed the Lord saying, "Commit all of your life to Me. Let go of those things you're holding on to. Don't go halfway on your spiritual journey—go all the way with Me."

Scenes from my life flashed before me. "Lord, help me to live the life You intend for me to live."

The winds howled, and the snow splattered all over the windshield. *Maybe I should pull to the side of the road and wait until morning. On second thought, I might get buried.* I cried out to the Lord again.

After seven eternal hours, I entered Sunriver around two in the morning. Snow blanketed the street signs, making them impossible to read. I got out of the car and whisked the snow off a street sign with an ice scraper. After doing this several more times, I found the lodge. When the door opened, my friend shouted, "Gail's here! We were so worried." Cheers erupted.

The following evening, a heart-wrenching story aired on the television news. A mother and child had been caught driving in the snowstorm and pulled to the side of the road. They were found frozen to death in their car.

The tragic news sent a shiver down my spine and broke my heart.

God used this ordeal to teach me a lesson to go all the way with Him in my spiritual journey—no matter how difficult the going gets. Never give up!

But the one who endures to the end, he will be saved. (Matthew 24:13)

~ Gail Kaku

அ ૐ ల

The Firestorm

A monstrous fire broke out in the hills of Oakland, California where my sister and her family lived. Upscale homes in a densely populated area on steep hillsides exploded into flames as hot, dry gusts spread the rolling inferno from neighborhood to neighborhood. Years of drought left an abundance of dead eucalyptus trees and dry vegetation that fueled the wildfire. Narrow, winding roads made it difficult for fire trucks to negotiate the hills, adding to the chaos.

My sister and her husband first heard about the catastrophic news on their flight home from a European vacation. Their children Kelly, eight, and Trina, five, were staying at my cousin's home near San Francisco.

When the news broke out, I quivered in fear and began praying. About two thousand people gathered at our church for a special service to pray for the Lord to stop the fire. Shortly after the prayer, the weather took a remarkable turn and shifted from scorching heat to rain. It wasn't long before the fire fighters snuffed out the blazing inferno.

After the plane touched down, my sister and her husband raced to our cousin's house to pick up the girls. Instead of a "Welcome home Mom and Dad," Trina greeted her parents with a desperate scream, "Cloudy's at home!" She bawled inconsolably for their pet bunny. They hustled across the Bay Bridge and found that the authorities had closed off all the main routes to their neighborhood. They found an alternate way through back roads. Their hearts hammered as they passed blocks of ravaged homes and charred trees. After many detours through the hilly roads, they reached their street. The fire had stopped a quarter mile from their home.

Just a couple of months earlier, my nieces had received Jesus at a weeklong children's camp sponsored by our church. During the firestorm, they cried out to the Lord to save Cloudy. This was a real test of their new faith.

When they arrived home, Trina and Kelly stormed to the atrium. "Cloudy! Where are you?" the girls shrilled.

"Cloudy—he's not here!" Trina cried. "Where's Cloudy?"

Kelly pointed. "Look, the cage is gone!"

Later they learned that the *au pair* had taken Cloudy to her friend's house when she evacuated. My nieces rejoiced and thanked God for saving Cloudy.

Several days later Trina climbed a high chair and gathered cans of abalone from the pantry. Each can cost over $25 each. She donated them with some coins to the fire victims. The lady at the donation center smiled at Trina. "Sweetie, thank you for your donation, but we can't take your cans of abalone. We'll take your money though. Thanks sweetheart."

What a compassionate five-year-old.

"Fear not, for I *am* with you; be not dismayed, for I *am* your God. I will strengthen you, yes, I will help you, I will uphold you with My righteous right hand." (Isaiah 41:10 NKJV)

~ Gail Kaku

ও ৡ ৶

Over the Summit

*O*n a cold, brisk winter morning outside a cabin in the Sierra Nevada Mountains, our friend's car failed to start. The starter groaned, "grrrr-grrrr-grrrr." *Surely a boost from my car battery will jump-start John's vehicle.*

I moved my car across the snow-covered driveway and parked next to his. I pulled the jumper cables from my trunk and clamped them to the battery terminals. I revved my engine while John cranked his ignition—nothing. Not even the "grrrr" sound.

After a few more futile attempts, I removed the cables and shut the hoods. "I guess we have to call a tow truck," I said.

Just then, John got out of his car and placed his gloved hand on the hood. "Jesus, touch this car and bring it to life. You know what's wrong . . ."

He's praying?

John got back into the car, turned the key, and *voilà!* The engine roared to life. I stared saucer-eyed in disbelief.

On another occasion, I was driving up a steep grade near the Grapevine on Interstate 5 when the car began to overheat. Warning signs to shut off air conditioners were posted along this stretch of the freeway. Although I didn't have the air conditioner on, the temperature needle climbed and approached "HOT." My hands grappled the steering wheel, and sweat formed on my forehead. I thought back to the time in the Sierras when John prayed for his car. *I'll try prayer. I have nothing to lose.*

"Lord, please help this car make it over the mountain!" I drew in a deep breath and noticed almost immediately the needle starting to decline. I blinked hard and couldn't believe what I saw.

Soon it settled into the normal operating range while climbing the steep ascent. I drove the rest of the way home, some 300 miles without a glitch.

I know it doesn't always work this way, but on these occasions, God chose to miraculously fix cars.

"The things that are impossible with people are possible with God." (Luke 18:27)

~ Bob Kaku

~ 𝓨 ~

The Timeshare

*T*urquoise waters lapped against Seven Mile Beach's fine white sands under incandescent blue skies. Neck deep in water as clear as a swimming pool, Gail gushed, "Look, I can see my toes! There's tiny fish skittering around."

Smiling, I donned my snorkel mask and fins and swam in the warm water while surrounded by bright coral and exotic fish.

We had first visited this gem of a beach on a one-day visit to Grand Cayman Island during a Western Caribbean cruise. This time we came back for a week's stay at the Holiday Inn, nestled on the widest strip of Seven Mile Beach.

Scenes from the movie *The Firm,* featuring Tom Cruise and Gene Hackman, were shot at both this hotel and the Hyatt down the street.

We milled through the shops in Georgetown, the capitol, and sampled the island's freshly baked Tortuga Rum Cake. *Yum!* Store items were quite pricey as one might expect in a tourist area. It felt even more expensive because one US dollar converted to roughly eighty cents in Cayman money. Cayman dollars used the same "$" symbol as US dollars, adding to the confusion.

Shops and restaurants displayed invitations to visit time-share condominiums and offered cash incentives. By the third day, Gail ceded. "Let's attend. The gift will defray some of our expenses." We signed up for a meeting, vowing not to buy.

A personable and glib salesman flashed a magnetic smile and chatted with us before launching into his spiel. He then took us on a tour to see the unit and the rest of the sun-splashed resort.

When we returned, he crowed, "Grand Cayman is the ultimate location, and I have the perfect, discounted timeshare for you." He leaned forward in his chair and asked us point-blank, "Do you want it?"

My mouth tightened, and I glanced at Gail who looked like she was about to say yes.

Seeing that we didn't answer right away, he added, "Talk things over in the lobby. Take your time and let me know."

We made our way to the lobby. "This sounds really good," Gail said. "Should we do it?"

"Ah, yeah . . . uh, no . . . I thought we weren't going to do this."

"Jesus, please guide our decision," she prayed. We looked at each other and reasoned, "Why not?"

We stepped back into the salesman's office. "We'll take the timeshare," I said. He flashed a high-voltage smile and shook our hands. We signed the sales contract and paid half of the total with our credit card.

We revisited the property later that afternoon. Gail peered through the front window facing the beach. "You can hardly see the ocean." Then it dawned on us that future developments will obstruct the view altogether. We sauntered across the street and were disappointed to see a rocky stretch of the beach littered with broken glass, cans, and bottles.

That evening I thumbed through the worldwide timeshare exchange catalog. "The trade properties seem to be in remote locations." I scanned the contract and became disenchanted. "This timeshare doesn't include a real estate deed and is strictly a club membership. I think we made a mistake."

"We shouldn't have rushed into this," Gail lamented.

The following morning, I called the salesman. "I'm afraid I can't rescind the contract," he said.

"But aren't we entitled to the three-day buyer's remorse period?"

"That only works in California. Grand Cayman is British territory."

Crestfallen, I put the phone back in its cradle. Gail and I joined hands and prayed. "Dear Lord, please help us out of this mess . . ."

I contacted the credit card company in New York City to cancel the charge, but they required a credit memo. Then I called the sales office again and asked for the owner.

"The only person who might rescind the contract is the business manager," the salesman said. "But he's away at a meeting in Las Vegas and isn't due back until tomorrow."

The following day, the receptionist answered the phone. "The business manager left Las Vegas, but he's stuck in Mexico with aircraft engine problems. Check back tomorrow."

"Engine problems?" Gail's mouth formed an oval. "What else can go wrong?"

In spite of our dampened spirits, we tried to make the best of it. That night we dined by the water's edge and listened to a live band playing reggae and calypso music. Gentle waves broke on the beach. We watched the sun descend into the sea, painting a kaleidoscopic sunset of saffron, fuchsia, and pinkish-orange colors.

The day before our departure, we prayed again, fully committing the situation into God's hands. An unexpected calm descended upon us. We toured the island one last time. When we returned to our room, the phone message light was blinking. "I bet that's the salesman," Gail said with excitement in her voice. I pressed the message button and sure enough, it was him.

"The business manager is back," the salesman said. "I scheduled an appointment for you to meet with him at ten o'clock tomorrow morning."

I put the receiver down with a glimmer of hope. "I can't believe it—we're having that meeting after all. That's just three hours before our flight home."

The following morning, the business manager shook our hands and warmly greeted us. He gestured for us to take our seats. "Why do you want out of the timeshare?" he asked in a professional manner.

We humbly explained our reasons.

After a long pause, he said, "I don't want to obligate you with something you don't want." He released us from the contract and returned our deposit.

Wow! Just in time, Lord!

Rise up and help us; redeem us because of your unfailing love. (Psalm 44:26 NIV)

~ Bob Kaku

Chapter 2   LIFE CHANGERS

God brings people, events, and situations into our lives to shape us and bring forth changes. He wants to give us a life of victory, meaning, and purpose.

྾ 𓅃 ྾

Radio Station KRLA

*D*uring my high school years, two of my classmates died of drug overdoses, leaving me in emotional turmoil. For months, a thick, black cloud hovered over me and seemed to follow me wherever I went. I questioned the meaning and purpose of life. *God, do you exist? Are you up there somewhere? Why am I here?*

Just recently I had read *The Cross and the Switchblade* by David Wilkerson, a true story about his life and belief in a personal God. Whenever he prayed, he received answers. Whenever I prayed, nothing happened, until . . .

I sat on the hardwood floor, leaning against my bed and listening to the popular Los Angeles radio station KRLA, which was having hourly call-in contests. If you happened to be the "nth" caller, you won a prize. I silently asked God, "If you exist, show me by letting me win." I shuffled over to the phone, dialed the number once, and heard the phone ring.

A lady answered the phone. "Congratulations, you're the tenth caller. You won a B. B. King album."

"I won?" My mouth froze wide open. After a short delay, I heard myself scream over the airwaves. *God heard my prayer?*

Moments later a disturbing thought jarred my mind. *You*

were just lucky! God doesn't exist. You were bound to win sooner or later.

"God, if you really exist, let me win again."

During the next round of the contest, I called again. The same lady answered the phone, "Congratulations, you're the seventh caller. You won the B. B. King concert tickets."

I won again? Twice in one day! I almost dropped the phone. Then a harsh voice blared inside me. *That was just luck.*

The next day that disdainful inner voice returned. *God doesn't exist. You're lucky.* A fierce tug-of-war ensued inside me. Lingering doubt prompted me to try it again. I gawked in utter disbelief when I won a third time—this time, a Traffic album.

I had periodically gone to a Christian church that a neighbor invited my family to. But I became bored and quit going when I started high school.

"God, do you want me back in church? If so, let me win the contest again." I shrieked when I won a fourth time—a pair of Traffic concert tickets.

The disc jockey announced, "Didn't you just win? For some reason, some people win more than once. It's so amazing!"

Within minutes that antagonizing voice shouted. *You're lucky! How can God be everywhere?*

That same day, I pleaded, "God, just one more time."

I was flabbergasted when I won a fifth time. The following week, I returned to church. During the service, I fidgeted in my seat, playing with my rings, twisting them off and on my fingers over and over again. *Church is a waste of time.*

After a month of this, I asked God, "Do you really want me in church? If so, let me win the contest one more time." That very afternoon, I tuned in, called the station, and won $100. Although I didn't feel like it, I continued going to church regularly.

Imagine winning five times in two consecutive days and then a sixth time one month later, having dialed only once each time. What are the odds of something like that happening in a large metropolitan area like Los Angeles?

Not until three years had gone by did I begin to have a clue what it was all about. When I started college, I met Chrislee, a born-again Christian. One day while we were walking out of class, she asked matter-of-factly, "Do you believe Jesus is the Son of God?"

"I'd have to think about it."

She probed, "Do you believe Satan exists?"

"Huh?"

"You know how there's good and evil operating in the world. The evil forces are ruled by Satan, the devil. It's that harsh, condemning inner voice."

Just then I recalled the antagonizing voice I had heard every time I won on the radio. "Oh, I've heard that voice before. That's Satan?"

Chrislee said with great aplomb, "The Bible says the devil prowls around like a roaring lion to keep people away from God."

"You believe in the Bible?"

"It's the living Word of God," she said. "God uses the Bible to speak to us. We can receive Jesus into our hearts, be forgiven for our sins, and spend eternity with God—or we can reject Him, die in our sins, and suffer eternal consequences."

I challenged her beliefs and asked many questions. For almost a year, Chrislee and her two brothers answered all my questions, showing me Bible references that supported their responses.

On Easter another friend invited me to her church. Toward the end of the service, the pastor gave an invitation to receive a life of promise and meaning in Jesus. I wanted that and wove my way to the front of the church. I recited a prayer with a

group of people and received Jesus into my life. An indescribable peace filled my heart.

I began to develop a personal relationship with Jesus as I
prayed and talked to Him. I met with other Christians and
began to grow in my faith.

God's transforming power began to change my thinking
and values as I studied the Bible. I renounced certain things I
had dabbled in—horoscopes, Ouija boards, hypnosis, fortune
telling and palm reading. I never knew these things were
offensive to God.

I became motivated not only in my faith, but also in other
aspects of my life. A college instructor asked, "What happened
to you? All of a sudden, you went from being a mediocre
student to doing exceptionally well."

When my grandmother came to visit us, she commented to
my mom, "There's something different about Gail. She's
beaming. What happened to her?"

Mom didn't know, but I did. I had found Jesus, the
beckoning light of my life.

"Lord I believe you allowed me to win so many times,
because I sincerely sought You with all my heart."

"You will seek Me and find Me when you search for Me with
all your heart." (Jeremiah 29:13)

~ Gail Kaku

കൗ ✣ ൭

A Time to Live

*D*uring the waning days of World War II, there lived a young girl in Kokura, a city on the island of Kyushu in south-western Japan. B-29s rumbled overhead, dropping incendiary bombs in her neighborhood. In one particular raid, explosives ripped holes into the street right in front of her house.

Little did she know that Kokura was singled out for an even more horrific weapon. It was the primary target for the world's second atomic bomb because of a large ammunition arsenal located there.

When the B-29 *Bock's Car* approached Kokura, thick haze and smoke prevented the crew from seeing the arsenal.

Just one day earlier, a large squadron of B-29s bombed the neighboring city of Yahata. A cluster of wooden houses near a large steel mill burst into flames, sending thick, billowing smoke over Kokura.

Explicit orders were given to the crew members to only drop the atomic bomb if the target could be seen. After three unsuccessful passes, the plane turned southwest toward its backup target.

The bomb killed an estimated 70,000 people in Nagasaki and ultimately caused Japan to surrender.

Several years after the war, the young girl grew up and married a Japanese American living in Japan. A couple of years after that, they had a baby boy. That young girl who survived was my mother, and I was that baby.

For You formed my inward parts; You wove me in my mother's womb. (Psalm 139:13)

~ Bob Kaku

෩ 𝒴 ෨

Second Chances

I've been hit by cars twice in my life.

The first time, I was riding my bike on the way to high school on the wrong side of a busy street when a car stopped perpendicular to me. The driver was looking away toward the oncoming traffic to turn right. He lurched forward and turned.

Bang! His car barreled into my bike, and I was thrust airborne and landed in a grassy vacant lot. Acute pain shot through my left knee.

The driver asked, "Are you okay, son?"

"My knee," I said in a weak voice.

He carried me into his car and rushed me to the hospital. I was treated for some bruises and sprained tendons in my knee. I hobbled around on crutches for a couple of weeks. Today, many years later, I still feel pain in that knee on cold days. But it could have been a lot worse.

Another brush with death occurred during my sophomore year at UC Berkeley. I spent all night working on a final essay. In the morning, I left the dormitory and headed over to campus to turn in the paper. On the way over, I waited on the corner of a bustling one-way, three-lane street. Cars in the nearest and farthest lanes stopped at the crosswalk. I proceeded.

When I reached the middle of the center lane, I saw something moving out of the corner of my left eye and turned to face it. A car appeared out of nowhere and sped toward me. In a nanosecond that seemed to pass in slow motion, I stood immobilized. Tires screeched as a Volkswagen Carmen Ghia bashed into my lower legs. *Wham!*

The impact hurled me up into the air, and I crashed face-first onto the hood of the car. *Thump!* Dazed, I peeled myself off the car. I tried to stand but collapsed. When I came to, I found myself lying on the sidewalk. A large crowd flocked around me. Blood streamed from my nose and mouth while some pedestrians waited with me for the ambulance.

Muffled sounds drifted in and out of my consciousness. A woman argued with a policeman. "He came out of nowhere! I couldn't stop," she snapped.

Sometime later, I noticed a student from my dormitory passing by. I cried out, "Bill." He turned to face me and was taken aback. "Turn in my final for me."

"Sure." He picked up the bloodstained pages littered in the street and headed to campus. A few weeks later, I received my grade and was surprised to receive an A. My professor must have thought I put my blood, sweat, and tears into it—literally.

We zoomed off to the emergency room with sirens blaring. While I was lying on the gurney, panic seized me, and I started hyperventilating. The doctor gave me a shot to calm me down. After extensive tests, the hospital held me overnight for observation and released me the following day. I sustained a broken nose, cut lips, two black eyes, and massive purple-blue bruises on my arms and legs.

I figured I was lucky—but was it really luck?

After graduating college, I started going to church to please my girlfriend.

One Sunday the pastor's sermon had a profound impact on me. "God not only loves you, but He likes you. He knows everything about your past, your thoughts, your misdeeds—and He still likes you." I couldn't fathom God loving me, but I could understand the concept of God liking me.

The pastor said, "If you want a life of significance and purpose, come forward." An inexpressible desire compelled me toward the altar.

"God is a God of second chances," he added. "When we repent from our sins, He forgives us no matter what we've done, and He gives us eternal life in heaven."

This differed from my Buddhist upbringing where I was taught there are no second chances or redemption from past mistakes. At the altar, I gave my life to Jesus and made Him my Lord and Savior.

The relationship with my girlfriend didn't work out, but the Lord used it to bring me into a relationship with Him. I no longer believed luck had anything to do with my accidents or relationships. I believe God orchestrated these events not only to save my physical life, but more importantly, to save my soul.

"For I know the thoughts that I think toward you," says the LORD, "thoughts of peace and not of evil, to give you a future and a hope." (Jeremiah 29:11 NKJV)

~ Bob Kaku

൙ 𝓨 ൙

Kelly Belle's Prayer

*O*ne picture-perfect February day, I had an exciting job interview at a posh restaurant with two executive managers from Rockwell. Dressed in crisp business suits, we entered the rich mahogany-furnished restaurant with high ceilings and an opulent ambience.

"Strategic planning is the ultimate, premiere job in information systems," one manager said. He had zoomed up to the restaurant in a bright-red Porsche and appeared very successful. "You'll be replacing me." I listened intently as I savored my sirloin sandwich.

Mike, the other manager, smiled. "I really like your resume. It tells me you're not afraid to try new things. When can you start?"

My software programming job at Northrop no longer challenged me. I wanted something new and exciting. This opportunity would really advance my career. *I'd love to work at Rockwell, but the seven AM start time bothers me.*

"I'd have to give my boss at least a two-week notice, but I need to think about this."

After we finished our lunches, Mike handed me his business card. "Call me if you're interested."

A few days later, I visited my sister's family in Northern California. My mind kept drifting back to the Rockwell opportunity. I lifted my five-year-old niece, Kelly Belle, by the waist and twirled her in the air. She burst into laughter and screamed, "Faster." After setting her down, we caught our breaths.

Kelly Belle wasn't her real name, but an affectionate nickname. I squatted down to her and looked into her large almond-shaped eyes. "Kelly Belle, ask Jesus if it's okay for me to work at Rockwell."

She smiled ear to ear, clasped her tiny hands together, and prayed. "Dear Jesus, is it okay if Auntie Gail works at Rockwell?"

That very night, the Lord spoke to me in a dream. "No, don't go to Rockwell. There are gold nuggets in staying at Northrop."

He not only answered Kelly's prayer, but He had much more to say to me. "You're pursuing the wrong men. Turn from your wicked ways."

I awoke startled and pondered the dream. Later that morning, I found Kelly playing with her toys in the family room. I stooped down toward her. "Gosh, Kelly Belle, your prayer was so powerful! Because of your faith, little girl, God already answered it and said no to Rockwell."

She shrieked, "WHY-Y-Y?"

"Gold nuggets await me if I stay at Northrop."

Kelly giggled and went back to her toys.

After I returned home, I asked the Lord, "What wicked ways must I turn from? I'm going to church, spending time with other Christians, praying, and reading the Bible. I'm even giving tithes and offerings!"

The Lord brought to mind some warnings I deliberately ignored about a relationship with someone I'll call Jeremy. He was a Christian in name only. God wanted me to let go of the relationship, because Jeremy wasn't a born-again Christian. I couldn't shake the verse:

> Jesus answered and said to him, "Most assuredly, I say to you, unless one is born again, he cannot see the kingdom of God." (John 3:3 NKJV)

I somehow knew the relationship was pulling me away from the Lord. But I was so enamored with him that I couldn't let go. I vacillated. *What if I never meet anyone like him? Can I really trust God?* God seemed to be telling me that my rebellion was wickedness in His eyes.

Not knowing what else to do, I sought counseling at my church.

The prayer pastor listened intently and looked at me with grave concern. "When we deliberately ignore God's warnings, our relationship with Him is broken, and we tread on shaky ground. Being a Christian doesn't give you a license to live any way you want. I want you to do a three-day, water-only fast. It will help you to rely completely on God. Often spiritual bondages are broken. Come back after your fast, and I'll pray for you."

"I never fasted before. Can it be a juice fast?"

"Okay."

The counsel disheartened me for weeks. I waited until a holiday weekend and fasted. I craved food and slept a lot to forget my hunger pangs and misery.

Sometime during this process, I made a decision. *Lord, I release Jeremy to you.*

My heart screamed with pain as if a dagger plunged into it.

A day or two later, I attended a Bible study at work. Sadness must have shown on my face because one of the Christian men walked over to me, held my hand and started praying for me. As he was praying, his hand began to tremble and heat surged from it. By the end of his prayer, all the emotional pain completely disappeared. God healed my heart!

I returned to my church and met with the prayer pastor. When he prayed for me, something uncanny happened. I had a vision and saw myself wearing an elaborate gold crown covered with brilliant diamonds. *What a beautiful crown! Why am I seeing this?* Suddenly the image changed, and Kelly Belle appeared, wearing that same crown with a mile-wide smile.

When I opened the Bible that day, I happened to land on the following Scripture:

> Praise the LORD, O my soul, and forget not all his benefits—who forgives all your sins and heals all your diseases, who redeems your life from the pit and crowns you with love and compassion (Psalm 103:2–4 NIV).

This is a crown verse!

I stared in awe and reread the passage several times. I began to apply it:

He crowns me with His love and compassion.

He forgives me for all my sins.

I had an epiphany. The verse confirmed that the Lord had forgiven me for my rebellion and restored me back into a loving and compassionate relationship with Him.

The crown on Kelly reassured me that God worked through this little girl to redirect me to the right path.

A few weeks later, I received a new and interesting software project at work.

This must be one of the "gold nuggets."

That summer I attended a Mount Hermon Christian conference for my vacation. That wouldn't have been possible had I taken the Rockwell job. It was there in the Santa Cruz Mountains that God led me to discover the real gold nugget, Bob, to whom I am now married.

The prayer of one little five-year-old changed my life forever.

"I am the LORD your God, who teaches you what is best for you, who directs you in the way you should go." (Isaiah 48:17 NIV)

~ Gail Kaku

ॐ ✌ ॐ

A Wave of Love

*B*ob pattered up the stairs into the bedroom where I was wrapping door prizes for a New Year's Eve party. "Your friend, Paul Tabe, and his family are in Phuket, Thailand," he bellowed. Just hours earlier, we had watched the harrowing news about the deadly tsunami triggered by the Sumatra-Andaman earthquake. Goose bumps formed all over my arms.

"No!" I shrieked. My heart raced with panic.

"I received an e-mail from Paul's friends in Holland. They want to know if we have his mom's phone number."

I had known Paul to be a kind and generous person ever since I met him in college. After some research, I found his mom's phone number and called. His mom answered the phone and said, "Paul called the day after the tsunami to say they're okay. But they're evacuating their bungalow. We haven't heard from him since. I'm so worried I can't sleep."

I hung up the phone not knowing whether to feel relieved or appalled.

Paul told me his story after he returned home:

"My family and I went to Phuket for a month-long vacation. My three-year-old daughter, Lana, and I were at the beach when we saw a strange phenomenon. The ocean receded far beyond the normal low tide. You could see fish flapping on top of the coral. Lana and I wandered out to have a closer look at this bizarre sight. Six other vacationers were also on the beach when someone yelled, 'This can be dangerous. It might be a tsunami.' We started to make our way off the beach. Around fifteen seconds later, I heard a woosh sound and saw in the distance a wall of water rushing in. I picked Lana up and clambered up a hill toward our bungalow just as the water slammed into the beach. We avoided the perilous wave by seconds.

"My wife and son were looking down from the bungalow balcony after hearing all the commotion. When I looked back at the ocean, the seawater had turned from a clear turquoise to a murky brown color with all kinds of floating debris. A Thai girl was having trouble keeping her belongings from floating away. She had been selling drinks on the beach earlier, and it represented her entire livelihood. I gave Lana to my wife and ran down the hill to help. The girl and I grabbed her heavy steel ice chest and held on. It saved us from being swept out to sea.

"A few moments later a second wave hit. Someone in the bungalow next to ours yelled, 'The restaurant's being destroyed.' I ran toward the restaurant to see if I could help. As I was passing a bungalow, the third wave struck. Water gushed into the bungalow and people inside were waist deep, trying to escape. I stopped to help them gather their belongings. Everything happened in a flash, and I couldn't think of anything except helping those in need.

"We stayed with the owner of the bungalow and restaurant complex who lived on a hill. They accommodated everyone. He and his family brought food and water to us every day. Their positive attitude and composure helped us cope with the great stress. Later, his family discovered two members of their extended household had died at another beach. Yet during their time of grief, they continued helping others.

"The morning after the tsunami, only five of us were available to start the massive cleanup. Later, some other tourists joined us. The floodwaters had completely leveled the restaurant, destroyed two bungalows, and damaged others. We did backbreaking work in blazing heat with no shade. We used our bare hands to pick up scrap metal, shards of glass, and other debris. We broke large slabs of concrete with a sledge-hammer. Amazingly, no one got hurt.

"The tsunami carried automobiles from the parking lot, tossing them like toys onto the beach. It took seven or eight people and a small pickup truck to haul each vehicle out of the sand. Heavy equipment couldn't get down the narrow hillside road. When we started the rebuilding, I mixed cement by hand and worked under primitive conditions.

"The work force eventually grew to fifty people and included a Belgian journalist who anchored his boat off our beach, Ao Sane. He raised 100,000 euros through his Web site and distributed the money to the local people who lost businesses and homes. An American couple also helped with the cleanup. They raised money through their church in Georgia and gave it to the restaurant owner to help replace tables, chairs, and other things.

"After three weeks, the restaurant was up and running and we departed for home. When we arrived at the airport, we were surprised to see a massive bulletin board listing a multitude of missing people. It wasn't until then that I realized how close to tragedy we had come.

"Just ten minutes before the tsunami, I was about to go snorkeling, but my daughter wanted to play at the beach. Had I gone snorkeling, I probably wouldn't be here today. I thanked God for sparing my life through my daughter.

"I'll never forget the incredible teamwork and overflowing love and support people gave each other during this desperate time. It brought fervent hope and was the bright spot in the midst of this great tragedy.

"This vacation turned out to be the most rewarding experience I've ever had."

The entire law is summed up in a single command: "Love your neighbor as yourself." (Galatians 5:14 NIV)

~ Paul Tabe as told to Gail Kaku

Chapter 3   THE LORD ONLY KNOWS

God knows everything about us—our thoughts, actions, words, and deeds. Yet He accepts us just as we are. He knows us better than we know ourselves.

ॐ 🕊 ༄

Eighty-seven Percent

*A*n ensemble of birds chirped outside my bedroom as I awoke cheerfully on a crisp, sunny morning. *Whew! I scored eighty-seven percent on my business midterm.* As I readied myself for school, bewilderment set in. *Wait, was that a dream?* Then reality struck me like a lightning bolt. *Yikes, I still have my midterm to take!*

I had a bad habit of procrastinating with my studies. My friends and I "studied" at one of the USC libraries known as a social hangout. There we spent hours chitchatting and taking long coffee breaks. Sometimes I didn't get past the first page of my reading assignments.

In the next two days before the test, I secluded myself at a library where no one knew me and crammed.

When the exam papers were graded and returned, I stared at my test score goggle-eyed with my mouth agape. Eighty-seven percent—just like my dream! Moments after that, I heard a soft inner voice say, "I knew your test score before you took the exam." *Jesus, is that You?*

When I became a Christian, I began to recognize His voice. His is mostly a faint voice I can hear only with my spiritual ears, not with my physical ears.

Wow! I had a God-given dream. When I read the Bible that day, the following verse tugged at my heart:

"But the very hairs of your head are all numbered." (Matthew 10:30).

He knows me better than I know myself. What a meticulous God!

"I am your Creator. You were in my care even before you were born." (Isaiah 44:2 CEV)

~ Gail Kaku

ॐ ᚩ ᚱ

Kimono

*A*ll the ladies dressed in *kimonos* at my cousin's wedding in Japan. Aunt Katsue loaned me a beautiful, embroidered silk *kimono* with a wide *obi* sash. She wrapped the *obi* around my waist several times and yanked it so tightly I could hardly breathe. I thought I was going to die. I put on *tabi* socks and slipped my feet into her wooden *geta* sandals.

The *kimono* reminded me of my childhood days when I danced with my sisters at Japanese festivals in Los Angeles, wearing colorful kimonos, and snapping *kachi-kachis* (wooden clickers) or waving folding fans.

During the wedding banquet, I started thinking about how miserable I was wearing the *kimono*.

Jesus help me!

At that moment, I remembered God had been teaching me to think like He does:

Finally, brothers, whatever is true, whatever is noble, whatever is right, whatever is pure, whatever is lovely, whatever is admirable—if anything is excellent or praiseworthy—think about such things (Philippians 4:8 NIV).

God not only wanted my mind to dwell on pleasant things, but also for my attitude to be more thankful to Him, no matter what circumstance I found myself in. As hard as it was, I made a conscious effort to do what He was teaching me. I began thanking Him for being with me and for caring about every situation.

As I was thanking the Lord, something unimaginable happened. Suddenly, I saw Jesus wearing a beautiful, indigo-print *kimono* in my mind's eye. The image vanished after a few seconds. *Jesus in a kimono?* I chuckled. Of course, He loves the Japanese people. He is God of all nations.

Just then, my aunt walked over to me and said, "You can change into your American clothes now." My eyes widened with surprise.

My gratitude must have allowed Jesus to intervene for me. He cared about my discomfort!

O LORD, you have searched me and you know me. You know when I sit and when I rise; you perceive my thoughts from afar. (Psalm 139:1–2 NIV)

~ Gail Kaku

჻ 🕊 ჻

Nihon (Japan)

*A*t a Buddhist temple near Kobe, my relatives bowed to man-made statues and images and waited expectantly for me to follow suit. I loved my kindhearted relatives, and I didn't want to be disrespectful. But Bible verses rang out loud and clear inside me.

> "You shall have no other gods before Me. You shall not make for yourself a carved image . . . You shall not bow down to them nor serve them" (Deut. 5:7–9 NKJV).

My parents had taken me to Japan for my college graduation gift so I could learn about my ancestral roots. Our relatives took us sightseeing all over, stopping at several of the temples that dot the countryside.

I had heard Buddha was a compassionate prince who forsook his palace to find the answers to human suffering and to escape the miseries of reincarnation. But the answers he got through meditation resulted merely in a religious philosophy that did not introduce him to the living God. Buddha was an agnostic who believed if there were such beings as gods, they had nothing to do with human affairs.

Although bowing to a man-made image seemed harmless, I knew it was a great offense before the living God. Many innocent people have been deceived into believing that all roads lead to heaven. In the Bible, Jesus says:

"I am the way, and the truth, and the life; no one comes to the Father but through Me" (John 14:6).

Wrenching sorrow and heaviness filled my heart as I watched my relatives bow to these statues. *Lord, if they only knew how much You love and care about every detail of their lives.*

I had learned that true Christianity isn't a set of rituals or a religious philosophy, but rather a personal relationship with Jesus.

Because of the language barrier, I couldn't explain to my relatives that my faith didn't allow me to do this. I didn't want to hurt anyone. Neither did I want to offend God, nor distance myself from Him. I reflected on a verse:

"But whoever denies Me before men, I will also deny him before My Father who is in heaven." (Matthew 10:33)

My heart pulsated. At the altar, I chose not to bow to Buddha—I would be denying Jesus.

Some of my relatives stared at me in stunned silence. My aunt looked at me puzzled. Mom scowled and chided me.

"But Mom, I distinctly heard Jesus tell me not to bow."

"We aren't worshipping Buddha by bowing but doing it for tradition's sake!"

"But the Bible says these "other gods" are idols and man-made doctrines controlled by Satan."

"Well, why don't you just bow to the relatives and not at the altar," Mom said.

"Okay, I can do that."

Deep inside me, I knew I made the right decision. I sensed a strong presence of the Lord for the remainder of the trip.

"They worship me in vain; their teachings are but rules taught by men. You have let go of the commands of God and are holding on to the traditions of men." (Mark 7:7–8 NIV)

~ Gail Kaku

~ ❦ ~

Zoom

With a roar, my Toyota Supra whisked around undulating and winding roads like an acrobatic plane twisting and turning. A light touch on the accelerator revved the powerful engine and sent me flying at high speeds in seconds.

Gail and I zipped off in this sports car decked out with crepe paper flowers, streamers, and the obligatory "Just Married" on the rear window.

In the months after the wedding, I parked my car in the driveway of our home. My "bachelor" furniture, an odd collection of mismatched hand-me-downs moved into the garage and took half the space. My Lido 14 sailboat consumed the other half and left no room for our cars.

"When are you going to clear out the garage?" Gail asked. "We need to park our cars in there."

"I've been meaning to do it, but something keeps coming up." *My car's safe with two alarms.*

Several months passed. For a while, Gail didn't say anything about the garage, but one autumn day, she reminded me again.

At last, I had a free weekend, and I threw on some old clothes and started to clear the garage. Within minutes, the

phone rang. Someone needed help with some church maintenance, and off I went.

Later that night, during the early morning hours, Gail
shook me awake. "Did you hear that noise?"

I squinted at the clock—a little after two in the morning.
Loud clanking sounds seemed to come from the roof. *Clank.
Bang. Clatter.* Our neighbor's dog howled away. An eerie
sensation came over me. "I'll go check outside."

"No, it could be dangerous."

We sat up for a while, but soon the noise subsided and we
succumbed to sleep.

The following morning, I stepped into the driveway.
Where's my car? Perplexed, I looked down the street first to
the left, then to the right. *Didn't I park in the driveway?* Then it
hit me. I made a beeline into the house and breathlessly
hollered, "My car's gone!" A chill pulsated down my spine.
Why didn't the alarms go off? An awful feeling of violation
pervaded me.

Gail flew out of bed and ran outside. "I can't believe it!"

Trembling, I called the police. When they arrived, an
officer asked me a few questions and jotted down notes.

"Auto thieves have been operating in the area and target
Supras for their parts," the first officer said. "They turn around
and sell them to unscrupulous body shops."

"Is that so?" I asked.

"I'm surprised the alarms didn't go off," Gail interjected.
"Bob had two alarms."

"Professionals can defeat alarms in a matter of minutes,"
the second officer explained. His comment surprised us.

The next day, I received a call from the police. "We found
your car abandoned about fifteen miles away and had it towed
to an auto body shop—"

"You already found my car? We'll be right down." I put
the phone down with resignation.

When Gail and I arrived, I identified my car and shuddered. I blinked hard and couldn't believe what I saw.

My poor car!

The doors, mirrors, velour seats, stereo, equalizer, and everything inside were completely stripped. The thief left just the steering wheel, engine, and tires intact so he could drive it to a location and dump it.

Sometime later I realized the Lord had tried to warn me through Gail when she repeatedly urged me to clean up the garage.

Boy, did I learn an expensive lesson!

Listen and hear my voice; pay attention and hear what I say. (Isaiah 28:23 NIV)

~ Bob Kaku

る ソ ぐ

Down and to the Right

*W*ith a glint in her eyes, Gail smiled. "The contractors did a great job!" At last, our two bathrooms were magically transformed into new ones. Bright ivory-colored tiles with a marble design snugly enclosed a new tub in one bathroom with a new floor. A new shower with a frameless glass door enhanced the aesthetics of the other bathroom, making it appear larger.

We selected some attractive chrome and gold-trim towel racks with matching toilet paper dispensers to accent the newly textured and painted walls.

I gathered my electric drill, ruler, level, and other tools from the garage to attach the decorative accessories. After carefully measuring the length of the first towel rack, I drilled the holes and installed the side brackets. Mingled scents of fresh paint and drywall dust permeated the area. When I tried to insert the towel bar, it didn't fit. *Hmm—the side brackets are too close.* I angled and maneuvered the bar in vain.

Gail checked in on me, rolled her eyes, and left the room.

I'll use my hacksaw to solve it. I took the towel bar to the garage and sawed a quarter inch off. I brought it back and tried it again. *There, it fits. I'll do a better job on the next one.*

To my chagrin, the second towel bar didn't fit either. *That's funny.* I thought my measurements were precise. This time, I took a half inch off.

Gail peeked in and saw me struggling with the third one. "You've been working on this all day. Didn't you say it would only take a couple of hours?"

"It's a lot harder than it looks," I fired back.

The following day, I continued with the remaining towel bars. I couldn't believe I ended up cutting all five. *At least they fit and are level.*

Now I had to install the toilet paper dispenser. This measurement had to be exact, because I couldn't saw the spring-loaded pin that held the toilet paper. After installing the side brackets, I slipped the toilet paper onto the pin. This time I had the opposite problem. The brackets were a bit too far apart. *But it'll work.*

Gail walked in and pointed. "It's crooked." She tapped the toilet paper roll with her hand, and it bounced to the floor. "You need to redo it."

"It's supposed to be like that! You put too much pressure on it!"

"No, I tapped it lightly. Now we're going to have extra holes on our freshly painted walls!"

I suppose I could fill the drill holes with spackling—but what a shame, it won't match.

Seething, I stormed off to the hardware store. *Doesn't Gail know I'm not a handyman?* As I was driving, I heard God speak to my spirit. "You're not just mad at Gail; you've been mad all week."

Is that You, Lord? I reflected on all the things that had gone wrong at the office, and how I lost my temper.

"Lord, I'm truly sorry for the way I've acted toward Gail and some people at work. Please forgive me. I promise to make things right with her and my colleagues."

The Lord spoke to me again. "Gail's right. You need to redo the toilet paper dispenser. And one more thing—move it down and to the right."

Huh? Move it down and to the right?

After I returned, I sincerely apologized to Gail and described my encounter with God.

"Wow! Jesus spoke to you?"

I unscrewed the left bracket and drilled the holes slightly *down and to the right*. When I refastened the bracket, the previous drill holes were completely covered. "Yes!" I placed the level on top of the dispenser, and the bubble indicator was right in the middle. I loaded the toilet paper, tapped it with my hand, and it stayed put.

Everything worked out perfectly.

In your anger do not sin: Do not let the sun go down while you are still angry, and do not give the devil a foothold. (Ephesians 4:26-27 NIV)

~ Bob Kaku

☙ 𓅃 ☙

Ouch!

*O*n a midsummer morning, I awoke squinting at the bright sunlight seeping through the slats of the window shutters. I rubbed my eyes and noticed blurred vision in my left eye. I blinked hard but it still didn't clear.

Maybe I have excessive mucus from allergies. I shut my right eye and noticed straight lines appeared crooked. *Whoa. Something's wrong!*

I scheduled an appointment with an ophthalmologist but couldn't get in right away. About that time, Gail took off with her friend to a revival near Fresno, California. Two days later, I joined her at a small church packed with people.

"Get prayer for your eye," she said.

I asked the evangelist to pray for my eye and high blood pressure problems.

He began praying for me and in the middle of the prayer he paused and said, "Your eye problem is connected to your high blood pressure." I shrugged.

Two weeks later, the ophthalmologist shined the retinoscope directly into my eye. I fought hard to keep it open. "Some of your blood vessels are hemorrhaging," she said. "Your eye problem is caused by high blood pressure."

I recalled the evangelist's words and told the story to her. She looked at me quizzically. "Is he a doctor?"

"No, I don't think so."

"You might need laser surgery. Schedule an appointment with the eye surgeon."

From everything I've heard, laser surgery is safe, quick, and painless.

A week later Gail and I, along with other guests, were enjoying a Japanese *ramen* noodle dinner at a friend's home. We gathered together to pray afterwards.

Gail leaned over and whispered in my ear, "I kept seeing a torch making contact with you. Every time it touched you, sparks of fire burst out, and you jumped. The images kept repeating themselves."

I grimaced.

On the day of my appointment, the eye surgeon ran some tests and looked at me glumly. "You need laser surgery immediately. Did you drive today?"

"Yes," I replied.

"Then we can't operate today. Have someone drive you here tomorrow. The treatment will repair the hemorrhaging blood vessels, clear up some of the blurriness, and prevent it from getting worse."

The following day, Gail drove me to the medical facility. The surgeon harnessed my head into the laser instrument and deftly shot several rounds of laser bursts into my eye. Every shot felt like a pinprick. After five minutes, my head began to throb like a base drum being pounded. I couldn't sit still. I could smell my flesh burning, and it nauseated me.

The nurse had given me a Tylenol 3 codeine pill earlier, but it gave no relief. The surgeon offered me an anesthetic shot in my eye. I shuddered at the mere thought of having a needle in my eye and declined. I held my head steady for the remaining fifteen minutes.

When Gail picked me up, I described my painful ordeal.

She gasped. "I wonder if the torch image represented the laser beam. Did you feel like jumping every time the laser shot you?"

"Yeah, I would have jumped if I weren't strapped in."

She chided herself. "We should have prayed for you before your operation."

That fall, we attended an art and wine festival in our hometown. Live bands played in the background and a pleasing barbeque aroma hung in the air. We stopped at a booth advertising *Lasik* surgery for vision correction. While Gail gathered some literature on the procedure, I conversed with a representative. "I've had my fill of laser surgery." I explained everything I had gone through.

The representative said, "It's a good thing you had your surgery. Without it you could have gone blind."

Gail and I stared at her thunderstruck.

As we strolled away from the booth, Gail gaped. "I know what the torch means. God tried to warn you to take action immediately!"

However, there is a God in heaven who reveals mysteries. (Daniel 2:28)

~ Bob Kaku

ॡ ॶ ॷ

Dee

A picture of a spinning roulette wheel with a bright-white ball rolling in the opposite direction appeared in my mind's eye when our fellowship group prayed for Dee. *How bizarre! Why am I seeing this?*

I didn't know Dee, but after the meeting, I approached her. "Dee, I saw a picture when we were praying for you." I told her about the roulette wheel.

She smiled enigmatically. "My husband and I don't gamble. He only does the stock market."

Her friend standing next to her chimed in. "Your brother gambles." Dee looked at me perplexed. We shrugged.

A few weeks later, I attended the meeting again and Dee was there. After the meeting I went to talk to her. "Dee, I saw more pictures. I saw sunrays streaming down from the sky. I believe it represents God's supreme power."

Her face lit up. "The sunlight is a good thing. It's the opposite of darkness."

"Then I saw someone with an elevated leg hooked up to an IV."

The whites of Dee's eyes grew conspicuously large and shock covered her face. "My brother Dikran is in the hospital with a leg infection due to complications from his kidney surgery. His leg is elevated. He's the brother who gambles!"

"Really!" My mouth froze wide open.

"I just came back from visiting him in the Los Angeles area."

I glanced at my notes. "I also saw a fishing boat in calm waters against the backdrop of an ancient village."

She flashed a knowing smile. "Oh, the fishing boat probably means seeking lost souls for Jesus. My brother isn't a Christian, and he needs salvation. I'm supposed to go back and pray for him."

"I saw one more picture. I don't know what it means but Jesus was sitting in the sky."

A few days later, I was reading the Bible and the following verses caught my eye:

> The LORD looks down from heaven; he sees all human-kind. From where he sits enthroned he watches all the inhabitants of the earth (Psalm 33:13–14 NRSV).

Jesus sits in the sky! How comforting to know that God is watching over Dee and her brother.

Dee flew back to Los Angeles and spent several months with her brother. When she returned, she told me what happened.

"I taught Dikran all about God's gift of salvation and explained, 'With the fall of Adam and Eve, sin entered the world. As a result, each of us inherited a sinful nature. But if you make Jesus the Lord of your life, He gives you eternal life in heaven with a resurrected body—you won't be sick anymore, and you'll be pain-free. Receiving Jesus is the most important decision you'll ever make.'

"I continued praying and reading the Bible to him. About a month later he said, 'I want what you have. What do I do?'

"I asked my brother, 'Are you ready to commit your life to Jesus?' He nodded. I was so happy. I read him a prayer and he recited after me:

Dear Jesus, I know I have broken Your laws, and I am truly sorry. Forgive me for my sins, and I repent from them. I believe You died for me, became resurrected, and live today. I invite You to become the Lord and Savior of my life. Fill me with the Holy Spirit so I can obey You, and do Your will for the rest of my life.

"I welcomed him into the Lord's family. He kept smiling. Then I got down on my knees, lifted my hands toward heaven and praised God for Dikran's salvation. He used to be an atheist. But now, he, too, was getting down on his knees, lifting his hands and praising God!

"The following morning he gushed, 'I heard Jesus say, "You're no longer alone. Don't be afraid, just listen to Me." '

"Sometime later my brother died."

When Dee told me the news, shock and sadness filled my heart. At the same time, I was very relieved that Dikran made his peace with God. I knew he went to heaven where he'll walk on streets of pure gold inside city walls decorated with jasper, sapphire, and every kind of precious stone.

Now I know why I saw the picture of the roulette wheel.

Jesus said to her, "I am the resurrection and the life; he who believes in Me will live even if he dies, and everyone who lives and believes in Me will never die. Do you believe this?" (John 11:25–26)

~ Dee Melconian and Gail Kaku

Chapter 4   ON THE JOB

Every day we can invite the Lord into our workplace. Jesus is an excellent business mentor and wants to be involved in our projects, decisions, and in every aspect of our work.

ᐓ ᐕ ᐖ

Enough Is Enough

*M*y caviar dream came true. With breathless excitement, I accepted the job offer from a very prestigious Fortune 500 company.

My colleagues and I dressed to the nines in stylish business suits. We worked a hectic pace in an impressive glass-clad high-rise in the heart of downtown Los Angeles. Managers presented me with achievement awards and promotions at marketing meetings held in luxurious hotels and country clubs.

The company consolidated four divisions into one, and I was assigned to a new manager. My job became even more demanding, and I worked long hours. After a year, the job grew old, and I wanted to transfer. A systems engineering manager extended me an invitation to join her group. Initially my manager approved the transfer, but later she changed her mind. I was livid and bit my lip to keep from screaming.

My manager promoted her favorites, whether or not they met their objectives. She overlooked minority employees like me, even though I met every objective. I resented her.

During this time, my prayers didn't seem to get answered. I poured out my frustrations to a prayer counselor at my church.

"You need to forgive your manager and ask for her forgiveness," the counselor said.

"But I'm the one who's been wronged, not her. Why do I need to ask for forgiveness?"

"If we hold on to animosity, it becomes like an incurable cancer that eventually destroys us. Don't let a bitter root grow inside you."

The following week my heart pounded when I met with my manager. "I'm a Christian, and I have a personal relationship with God," I stammered. "I feel my relationship with the Lord is hindered because I'm harboring a lot of anger toward you. Please forgive me for this."

She looked at me startled. "Of course, you have my forgiveness. What you've done is very admirable."

As I was walking out of her office, all the pent-up anger and resentment I had carried for over a year vanished. Poof—gone!

The company reorganized again, and I was assigned to another new manager and job.

As I sought the Lord, He gave me special insights for understanding complex computer configurations that allowed me to accurately forecast revenue. Even so, I wasn't happy in my new position, and I wanted to pursue my transfer to systems engineering.

My new manager will support it since the company places a lot of emphasis on career development.

During a one-on-one meeting with my new manager, I talked about my career goals and raised the subject of my transfer. I couldn't believe her response. "The needs of the business come first. You're needed in your current job." My heart nearly stopped.

To make matters worse, she split the workload of a colleague who kept missing forecast and dumped half of it on me. I gawked in utter disbelief when she did this.

Managing a monthly forecast of $2 million was already a daunting task. It left me with very little time to go out on dates or be with my friends. With the increased workload, my $2 million monthly forecast shot up to an unprecedented high of $3 million. Everyone else averaged $2 million.

It wasn't just me, but several people had developed stress-related symptoms. One colleague griped, "I can hear cracking sounds in my neck." Another colleague whined that the stress was causing his jaws to lock up.

"I can't take on more!" I said to my manager.

When my plea went unheard, I seethed like a teakettle about to boil over.

That's it! I'm handing in my resignation . . . No, chill out. Don't make a rash decision.

I decided to stay put. Even though I wasn't a morning person, I went to work at five AM whenever I had a forecast to prepare. Anyone missing their numbers had to deliver grueling, time-consuming presentations before the branch manager to explain what went wrong. I made sure I never had to do one.

Where are you, Lord? Why aren't you answering my prayers?

God graciously allowed me to make every one of my forecast goals. After an extraordinary and exhausting month, I was shell-shocked when my manager took 75 percent of another person's workload and foisted it on top of my mammoth load. I pushed back, but to no avail. Tears fell like raindrops.

I sought counseling at my church again. Another counselor listened to my plea and heard two words from the Lord: "occupy" and "endure," he said.

"I'm supposed to stay there?" My eyes became watery, and my voice began to crack.

"God won't leave you there forever. He always delivers His people."

"But you don't understand—I just cannot deal with my manager or the stress . . ."

"Pray for her."

I almost choked.

The counselor looked at me with compassion. After a long pause he said, "God gives us a choice. I believe He's calling you to stay in your current job. But if you're that miserable, it's okay to quit." I let out a big sigh of relief.

The counselor prayed for me and jotted Hebrews 11:27 on a little piece of paper and handed it to me.

When I arrived home, I looked up the verse:

> By faith he left Egypt, not fearing the wrath of the king; for he endured, as seeing Him who is unseen.

In bewilderment I read the verse again. *What does this have to do with my job?*

The counselor's prayer gave me some relief, and I returned to work. My monthly forecast now shot up to fifteen categories instead of the three that I started with. The monthly dollar volume skyrocketed to $5 million, boosting my stress with it. Now, the added pressure could blast me through the roof.

Despite the overwhelming workload and new customers, God gave me strength, and I had another phenomenal month and made my goals in all fifteen categories.

The following month, my manager presented me with a large trophy and merchandise award at our regional meeting. Among the fine gifts, such as skis and bicycles, I chose a Nikon FE2 camera.

Oh, whoopee. It didn't fix anything. I was still very disconsolate.

A few days later, I rushed into my manager's office to brief her on a family emergency. "The doctors found cancer in my mom and have to operate immediately," I said in anguish.

"She's scheduled for surgery today; I need to take the afternoon off."

"No! You can't have the afternoon off," she replied in a terse tone.

"Wh-aat?" Her words stung like a snake bite.

"Every time you go somewhere you leave work unfinished in my lap."

I bolted from her office. *That's it! I can't take anymore of this. Just what did she mean by I leave work unfinished in her lap!* Then it hit me. *She's still mad about the time I wouldn't let her send work packages to me during my vacation to a Mount Hermon retreat.*

I called my sister, a human resource specialist at another company. "I've had enough! I'm putting in my resignation today."

"No, don't quit. Remember Dr. Shigekawa had concerns about your stress? Go on a medical leave." It seemed discomfiting to me, but not knowing what else to do, I took my sister's advice.

During my time off, my manager made harassing calls to both my doctor and me. "Eight weeks is excessive time off!" she barked.

"You're not a doctor. Who knows—it could be longer," Dr. Shigekawa replied.

At the end of the eight-week period, I got into a car accident that extended my leave another month. Then I caught strep throat on the day I was due back and called in sick. My manager wouldn't accept my legitimate excuse and sent a taxi over to pick me up.

During my leave, I carefully re-evaluated my career goals. Prestige, money, and job all faded in importance. *Put God in first place!* He doesn't want me consumed in a job filled with torment that hindered my relationship with Him. After pondering the pros and cons, I decided to resign.

While riding in the taxi, I thought about how everything would play out. The mere thought of facing my manager triggered a flood of emotions—hurt, rage, bitterness, and fear.

I was reminded of a verse I tried so hard to forget.

"And when you stand praying, if you hold anything against anyone, forgive him, so that your Father in heaven may forgive you your sin" (Mark 11:25 NIV).

I looked out the window of the taxi as freeway signs flew by. At that moment, I prayed, *Okay, Lord—You've forgiven me for much. I choose to forgive her. I release the venom.*

My manager wore a sullen expression and shook my hand when I turned in my resignation. My colleagues cried when they heard the news.

A day or two later, I landed a good job offer from another company. When I read the Bible that day, my eyes transfixed on the verse that the counselor had given me sometime before. When personalized, it read:

By faith *Gail* left *her job*, not fearing the wrath of the *manager*; for *she* endured, as seeing *Jesus* who is unseen.

Jesus—You were there all along!

"I have watched over you and have seen what has been done to you in Egypt. And I have promised to bring you up out of your misery" (Exodus 3:16–17 NIV)

~ Gail Kaku

છ ૐ ৶

Tempting Offer

*D*uring Silicon Valley's "red hot" job market, I interviewed with a few companies and landed a couple of job offers. The first offer came from a high-flying software company, a quintessential Silicon Valley success story, which offered me a good salary and attractive benefits with stock options.

The hiring manager eased back in his chair and flashed a roguish grin. "You'll become very rich in a few years." The company's stock soared to record highs, turning regular employees into multimillionaires overnight. *Fortune Magazine* ranked this company as one of the best to work for. The financial incentives enchanted me.

After a few years, I may never have to work again.

The second offer came from an established company with a good reputation. They also offered a good salary with stock options, but it didn't seem as exciting or lucrative.

A few days later, Gail was reading the Bible, and the following verse struck a chord:

Do not wear yourself out to get rich; have the wisdom to show restraint (Proverbs 23:4 NIV).

She didn't feel comfortable about the software company and wanted me to work for the established company. We prayed for the Lord's guidance.

Gail called a former colleague who had worked at the software company for a year. She told Gail, "If you want to become very rich, this is the company to work for. But the environment is extremely brutal. It's a place to work for a while, make a lot of money off the options, then move on."

I wanted to know more so I called Gail's colleague. "I worked all the time," she said. "My typical work day started at six in the morning and finished around nine or ten at night. At five PM I drove thirty miles one-way to pick up my kids at day care. Then I dropped them off at home and drove all the way back to the office to work several more hours. Everyone worked on weekends. If you didn't put in these extra hours, the company laid you off." I became more and more disheartened as I heard her story.

I heeded the warning and took the other job. The established company turned out to be a good place to work with interesting projects and generous bonuses.

Six months later, high-technology companies were greatly distressed in the economic downturn that followed the boom. The software company had a sizeable layoff, and the market price of the stock plummeted far below the exercise price for the options I would have received.

God protected me from making the wrong choice.

"For what does it profit a man to gain the whole world, and forfeit his soul?" (Mark 8:36)

~ Bob Kaku

❧ 🕊 ❧

Vindicated

*M*oney and power seemed to matter most at the Silicon Valley company I worked for. People shot verbal bullets at one another, and outbursts flared frequently. One or two people left our department monthly to work for other companies.

A software developer erupted like a volcano when I found problems with his code. His manager never researched the situation and slandered me behind my back with scathing accusations to his boss, an executive manager.

My insides screamed when the executive manager downgraded my performance rating and took away my raise. "I never had a bad review before! Why didn't anyone bother to hear my side of the story?" I asked my manager. "The code had problems!"

I submitted a rebuttal, but nothing came of it. I began interviewing with outside companies and was deluged with calls during the hot job market. Just before making a job change to another company, I prayed for the Lord's guidance.

Don't run from your problems.

"Wh-aat? Is that the Lord telling me to stay?"

Night after night I cried myself to sleep. God reminded me that my battle wasn't with people.

A prayer I once heard came to mind. "I come against the power of politics . . ." As difficult as it was, I decided to trust God and stay in my current job. I began praying for the work environment and took the following verse to heart:

> We are not fighting against humans. We are fighting against forces and authorities and against rulers of darkness and powers in the spiritual world. (Ephesians 6:12 CEV)

I inserted the names of people who gave me grief into the verse. *Lord, I know this battle isn't with people; but rather a spiritual one.*

After persevering for a season, another opportunity arose within another department, and I transferred. I thrived in my new position and worked on many interesting assignments. My new boss was pleasant to work for, but his boss happened to be the one who downgraded my performance rating.

Around that time, a guest speaker at my church said, "Some bosses are going to approve promotions, bonuses and raises. They won't know why they're making these approvals, but it's because of a higher power." The words resonated within me, and I claimed it as a promise from God.

A few weeks later, my boss called me into his office. When I walked in, he shook my hand. "Congratulations! You've made all your milestones," he said with a 100-watt smile. "I'm awarding you with a milestone bonus."

"What a pleasant surprise!"

"Since you've completed all your software training, you're also being awarded a key technology bonus."

"I am?"

"Yes, and if you stay with the company, you'll receive bonuses every six months," he said magnanimously.

"That's great news!" I said in stunned amazement.

"Wait, there's more. I'm also promoting you."

"You are? Christmas is ahead of schedule this year."

He laughed and handed me my new compensation report that included a substantial increase. "Finally, you're going to receive the maximum profit-sharing check."

I stared slack-jawed and thanked him for everything.

The executive manager who had taken away my raise earlier approved all of these increases.

God fulfilled His promise to me.

For promotion and power come from nowhere on earth, but only from God. (Psalm 75:6 TLB)

~ Gail Kaku

Chapter 5   THE LORD CARES

God cares about every aspect of our lives and wants to be involved in everything we do, large and small, complex and simple. Nothing is too difficult for Him.

≈ ✣ ∾

Merci Beaucoup

*M*ost people who travel to Paris visit the Eiffel Tower, Champs Elysées, and the Arc de Triomphe. I managed to miss these renowned attractions, but I did some sightseeing at the Louvre Museum and Notre Dame Cathedral.

Just a few days earlier, my travel companion, Ginny, and I were basking under the Mediterranean sun, taking a respite from a whirlwind of travel to ten countries in nine weeks—changing venues every one to three days.

"My money's about to run out," Ginny said. "I'm going back to Germany to find a job."

"Hope you find something, Ginny. When you return to the States, let's swap photos. I'll see you."

From Greece, I continued alone to the French Rivera for a few days and then to Paris.

I lugged my heavy backpack into the Gare de Lyon train station and searched corridor after corridor for a vacant locker. I must have looked helpless because a Frenchman who didn't speak any English gestured for me to come toward the stairs. Normally, I wouldn't have responded to a stranger's hail, but I was so desperate; I didn't know what else to do.

My whole body tensed as I ascended the stairs with him.

Where are we going? Why am I doing this?

When we reached the top of the stairs, I was surprised to see vacant lockers galore. *Eureka!* He helped me stow my heavy gear into a compact locker.

I had some mail to pick up at the American Express office but didn't know how to get there. I showed the Frenchman the address. He motioned with his hands to follow him out of the train station.

We ambled through the city streets, passing an array of charming shops, quaint hotels, and historic sites. Without warning, he stopped at a café and gestured that we should eat. Being somewhat hungry, I walked in with him.

The waitress handed us a menu in French. *Croissant* and *pomme frites* "french fries" were the only words I knew. I pointed to an item I thought was a hamburger. When my food arrived, I was shocked to see a breakfast meal with eggs. After we finished eating, the Frenchman paid for my meal and wouldn't accept any money from me.

We traveled a few more blocks to an empty American Express building. A new address appeared on the glass door. *Oh, no, they moved?* The Frenchman flagged down a taxi and rode with me to the new location. When we arrived, he paid for the taxi and once again refused my money. I thanked him for everything and waved *au revoir* as I stepped into the American Express office.

This gentleman's kindness overwhelmed me. I didn't even know his name. *Was he an angel?*

The LORD, before whom I have walked, will send His angel with you to make your journey successful (Genesis 24:40)

~ Gail Kaku

Waimea Angel

On a brilliant, blue-sky day, I angled my Olympus camera for the best panoramic view of Waimea Canyon on the Hawaiian island of Kauai. Its crags, buttes, and deep river gorges in earthen hues of rose, lavender, pale green, and sienna ensured that Waimea lived up to its reputation as the Grand Canyon of the Pacific.

I leaned against the steel rail and pressed the shutter button. Suddenly, my leather camera case slipped from my hands, tumbled end over end, ricocheted off the ledges, and careened down the canyon wall. “Nnnoo!” I shrieked as I watched it come to rest in some shrubbery.

Now the lens will get scratched on this expensive camera Dad gave me!

My sister Pauline, some friends, and I were vacationing in Kauai. Our friend Curtis, who lived there, took us sightseeing all over, making stops at cascading waterfalls, stretches of pristine beaches, and the resplendent Waimea Canyon.

Just before some choice words flew out of my mouth, I was reminded of a book I had recently read, Merlin Carother’s *Power in Praise*. Merlin looked for the good in all situations regardless of the circumstances he found himself in; then he praised God. He believed praise activated God's power and blessings. Conversely, he believed negative thoughts and complaints stifled God's plans and led to defeat.

Not knowing what else to do, I decided to try it. I praised the Lord for being a God who cared about all things. I praised Him for understanding my dilemma. I praised Him for being all-powerful . . .

Suddenly, a young boy ducked underneath the guardrail and started making his way down the canyon to where my camera case rested. My eyes bulged, and I stared openmouthed when he retrieved it, clambered up the canyon wall, and handed me the case. I was flabbergasted.

"Behold, I am the LORD, the God of all flesh; is anything too difficult for Me?" (Jeremiah 32:27)

~ Gail Kaku

ॐ ॐ ॐ

Stalked

A leering, scary-looking guy followed me from across the street as I walked home from high school. He called out to me using obscene language. If I slowed, he slowed. If I accelerated, he accelerated. Stark terror gripped every fiber of my being and rippled through me.

Just two more blocks to home.

The stalker ran ahead of me, then crossed over to my side of the street. He stopped on the very street I had to turn on and waited. My heart hammered. I intentionally turned on the block before my street to try to trick him. I waited about five minutes, then tiptoed back to the intersection. When I looked down the street, my heart nearly stopped. *He's still there!*

"GOD HELP ME!"

I may have brought this plight upon myself with the type of clothes I wore. Mom had fits. "You're wearing that!"

Without thinking, I started down the street parallel to mine when something compelled me to start sprinting. Although I've never been much of a runner, on that day I ran like a gazelle. After passing nine or ten houses, my head turned left toward a driveway. Behind this house, I saw the top of our large, steel swing set that towered above the fence.

I bolted down the neighbor's driveway into their backyard. A white wooden fence divided their yard from ours. I scampered up the three wooden rails, hoisted myself over the fence, and landed in my mom's vegetable garden.

Many years later, I realized God showed me this alternate route and brought me home to safety.

Listen to my cry, for I am in desperate need; rescue me from those who pursue me, for they are too strong for me. (Psalm 142:6 NIV)

~ Gail Kaku

ॐ ꙮ ꙩ

The Surgeon

*D*uring my bachelor days, I zipped around in a spiffy sports car that had a powerful engine, sleek lines, and cool-looking retractable, pop-up headlights. One day a headlight bulb burned out, so I bought a replacement. I removed the old one and placed the new bulb inside the headlight housing. Before securing the bulb, I flipped the switch to test it. The headlight flipped down into the well, and I heard a clunk.

Uh, oh!

I forgot that with this type of headlight, the switch not only turns the light on and off, but also flips the headlight up and down into the interior well. I turned the switch off, and the bulb fell out.

I flicked the switch back on, and the headlight got stuck with the bulb lodged inside. I put my hand in through the tight gap and scraped my knuckles trying to loosen the bulb. It still wouldn't budge.

After struggling for over an hour, I loosened the bulb and placed it into the headlight. There was one problem. I couldn't put the screws in without the headlight in the upright position. If I let go, the bulb would fall out again, and I couldn't get to the switch on the steering column.

More time passed. It finally dawned on me to pray.

Exasperated, I cried out to the Lord to help me. Shortly after praying, a thought entered my mind. *Hold the bulb in with masking tape.*

Huh? Masking tape?

I went into the house, found a reel of masking tape, and tore off a piece. I taped the bulb to the headlight housing and flipped the switch again. Yes! It works. What a simple, but ingenious idea. *That had to be God.*

I fastened the screws and removed the tape.

When my housemate came home, I told him everything that happened.

"You used masking tape?"

"Yeah, it was all so amazing. Uh, wait a minute. Did I leave the screwdriver in the headlight well? Oh, no!"

He laughed so hard his stomach hurt.

My housemate recounted this experience a few years later when he roasted me as the best man at my wedding reception. He embellished the story by saying, "Bob wanted to become a surgeon at one time. Can you imagine Bob operating on a patient and leaving a scalpel inside the body?"

"For You are my lamp, O LORD; And the LORD illumines my darkness." (2 Samuel 22:29)

~ Bob Kaku

అం 🕊 ఆ

Nana's Birthday Cake

*7*he dramatic ocean vista blended with the cerulean sky when we arrived in Malibu, a popular coastal town lined with inviting shops and trendy restaurants. Gail had decided on the spur of the moment to take her mom, Nana, out to dinner for her birthday on a bustling Labor Day weekend. Four of us, including Gail's dad, Mas, arrived in town late Saturday afternoon.

Restaurants were already crowded at five o'clock as we cruised up and down Pacific Coast Highway. We didn't have reservations. We didn't have a restaurant selected. We didn't have much time. Mas, a diabetic, had to eat at regular intervals, or he'd become sick from low blood sugar. He had already grown weak.

"Just stop anywhere," he pleaded. "A hamburger is okay."

"Jesus, please guide us to a restaurant," Gail cried out. I was about to drive into a hamburger stand when she said, "Let's find another place. We can order some appetizers for Dad while we wait for a table."

At that moment, a waterfront restaurant came into view. Gail pointed. "Let's go there."

I rolled my eyes. *We'll never get in there.*

We pulled into the packed parking lot, and Gail jumped out of the car to put our names on the waiting list. We maneuvered our way into the crowded restaurant. "It's a ninety-minute wait," she hollered.

Before we had a chance to order appetizers, the hostess said to Gail, "A booth just opened up. Do you want it?"

Her face became animated. "Yes! We'll take it!"

The hostess seated us in the terraced dining room where every table had a spectacular ocean view. Aromatic scents of steak and seafood permeated the air.

A few minutes later, the waitress brought a variety of steamy, freshly baked breads to our table. Mas began eating immediately.

Thank God! He's out of danger.

After we finished our scrumptious dinners, another waitress whizzed past our booth to a nearby table carrying a large piece of mud pie with a candle aflame. The party at that table burst out singing, "Happy Birthday."

"I wish I could have a birthday cake," Nana said.

We told her we'd order one for her. But before we even had a chance to place the order, out of nowhere our waitress brought the same cake to our table.

"Who ordered the cake?" I asked.

We looked at one another nonplussed.

The waitress couldn't have heard Nana over the din of the packed restaurant with the music blaring and people singing. No one had ordered it. *Did an angel order this cake?*

The sun began to set over the shimmering waters as we walked out of the restaurant. A cool breeze from the Pacific Ocean blew on us as we watched the waves crash upon the rocky cliffs. God's dramatic beauty surrounded us as the sunset changed into a myriad of hues from golden yellow, dusty rose to vermilion that flared out over the ocean horizon. What an awe-inspiring panorama!

"God is so faithful," Nana said. "What an extraordinary birthday!"

You will be blessed when you come in and blessed when you go out. (Deuteronomy 28:6 NIV)

~ Bob Kaku

Dad

A shrill ring roused us in the middle of the night. Bob rolled over to his nightstand and answered the phone. A shivery dread coursed through my veins. I squinted at the clock—a little after one in the morning. Something was wrong. Bob somberly said, "Your father died."

Piercing pain exploded inside me, and my stomach tightened into a knot. A stifling wave of grief swept over me, and I burst into tears.

Memories of Dad flooded my mind. He was a quiet man who loved to eat tasty foods. He was hardworking and honest. Whenever he told my two sisters and me he was going to take us somewhere, he kept his promise. He taught us to be thankful if someone gave us a gift or did something nice. He taught us to save our money and spend it wisely.

When I was almost three years old, I poured a bottle of baby oil onto the linoleum floor of the den and used a cloth diaper to spread the oil around. "Let's go ice skating," I said to my older sister. We glided on the oiled floor with our shoes and had the time of our lives. "Wheee!" When the door flung open, Mom shrieked, and we ran for cover. But Dad remained calm and chuckled.

He loved to entertain guests from Japan and welcomed everyone. Guests sojourned at our Los Angeles home throughout the year, including one person who stayed two years. Dad took everyone to Disneyland, Knott's Berry Farm, Hollywood, Universal Studios, and other major attractions. Sometimes he visited these places seven or eight times a year depending on how many guests we had.

When Dad was in high school, Japan attacked Pearl Harbor. He was among 110,000 Japanese Americans living on the West Coast who were forced to evacuate to internment camps. Cars sold for $20 and refrigerators for $1 each. Many of them lost everything except what they could carry in a suitcase.

Only once after many years did Dad talk about his camp experience when we were driving home from Lake Tahoe.

"Barbed-wire fences enclosed the fairgrounds at a temporary camp in Turlock, California. I shared a barrack with Uncle Kaz, my high school friend Ben and his brother. Aunt Chiye's family of eleven was crammed into a single, smelly horse stall."

"Oh, my God!"

"Guards pointed guns at us from high watchtowers."

"Yikes!"

"About three months later, we were transferred to Gila, Arizona, a camp in the vast, harsh desert. This place was in the middle of nowhere and didn't have barbed-wire fences. Instead, soldiers patrolled the area in Jeeps around the clock. We survived scorching summers and freezing winters. There were Gila monsters, rattlesnakes, and scorpions."

"What's a Gila monster?" I asked.

Dad made a contorted face. "They're big ugly pink-beaded poisonous lizards, about three feet long."

"Yuck! Gross."

"A year later, we were transferred to Tule Lake for two more years."

Japanese Americans continued to face bitter discrimination after the war. Many of them weren't given opportunities for good jobs, even with degrees from top universities.

Now I knew why I grew up in a predominantly Japanese neighborhood.

After the war, Dad enlisted in the US Army. He attended a military intelligence language school in Monterey. He was later sent to Saitama-ken, Japan as a translator and interpreter for two years where he became a master sergeant. Upon discharge, he went to college with the GI Bill money. Later, he met Mom through mutual friends and married within a year.

Dad enjoyed cooking and made it his vocation. He owned and operated *White Castle,* a family-run restaurant that served sizzling T-bone steaks and a cornucopia of culinary delights. His customers savored the daily specials of tantalizing beef stew, cabbage rolls stuffed with meat, fluffy tempura, and piquant curry rice.

While Dad lived a fulfilling life with his job and family, he didn't know Jesus. For years I prayed for his salvation. Finally, one evening, Dad received Jesus into his life at a Full Gospel Business Men's banquet. I celebrated when he came back to the dinner table beaming. He started to attend a Japanese Christian church and was water baptized. He helped with building maintenance and cleanup. One Sunday my sister told me, "Dad forgot his offering and drove all the way home to pick it up." *Sounds like something he would do.*

Mom threw a special birthday party for him when he was about to turn seventy-seven. I didn't go because of a work deadline. Instead, I talked to him by phone. "I'm going into a nursing home the day after the party," Dad struggled to say. I was speechless. He had suffered from diabetes and poor health over the past eleven years. Mom had been his caregiver but could no longer manage. I didn't know it at the time, but Dad was saying, "Good-bye."

After two weeks in the nursing home, Dad caught pneumonia and was rushed to intensive care. When I went down to LA, he wasn't doing well. Two days later, he showed signs of improvement, and I returned home to the Bay Area. A few days after that, he died. It was like the lights went out.

Some time later Bob urged, "Let's go skiing. It'll help you through the grieving process." I didn't want to go but forced myself and went.

Usually I'm able to "schuss" down the slopes, but I kept stopping on every run. I could feel the warm tears rolling down my cheeks and the frosty air blowing against my face. Extreme sorrow and relentless pain lingered inside me. *How could I have missed Dad's birthday party? Where were my priorities?*

At midday I stood atop a mountain and cried out to God. "Please take away my pain." A brief moment later, I noticed the sunrays streaking through the snow-covered trees, and the rich blue sky shimmering in increasing brilliance. An indescribable serenity pervaded me. I knew God heard my prayer and dampened the pain. From that point on, I had a better grip on my emotions.

Miss you, Dad.

You keep track of all my sorrows. You have collected all my tears in your bottle. You have recorded each one in your book. (Psalm 56:8 NLT)

~ Gail Kaku

⮫ 🕊 ⮪

Hot Soup

*7*oward the end of a busy workday, my body ached all over. I shivered in my office as though I were inside an Eskimo igloo. I wiped the cold sweat beading on my forehead. The room wasn't cold. I called Gail to tell her I wasn't feeling well. "Come home early," she said. But I had a ton of work to do and went home at my usual time.

A whiff of aromatic chicken soup wafted through the kitchen as I walked in. Gail had prepared some zesty soup from scratch with chunks of tender chicken, fresh vegetables, rice, and flavorful spices. "Mmm." I filled up with a second serving. A few minutes later, I began to perspire. I shuffled over to the medicine drawer and grabbed a couple of Tylenol capsules. I took only a few steps before a whirling sensation came over me. Suddenly, everything around me began to fade. My legs gave out, and I blacked out. *Thump!*

In my next conscious moment, I found myself lying on the kitchen floor, dazed with the Tylenol capsules scattered next to me. Gail panicked. "What happened to you?" She grabbed my arms but didn't have the strength to pull me up.

I braced myself against the kitchen island and pulled myself up. As I tried to walk, everything around me darkened again. I awoke when my head conked the wood floor, and I lay semiconscious for a while. Gail shrieked. "You scared me to death! Don't try to walk on your own again. Here, grab my shoulder." I gingerly got up with her help and plopped onto the sofa in the family room. "We need to rush you to emergency!"

Just then the doorbell rang. Our friend Dave came over to pick up Gail for a class. She had canceled the ride earlier, but he hadn't received her message in time. He helped me into our car, and Gail dashed off to the emergency room.

The doctor placed a stethoscope on my chest and listened to my breathing. I told her everything that had happened, including what I ate for dinner.

"When you have a viral fever, drinking hot soup or doing anything to elevate your body temperature is absolutely the wrong thing to do," the doctor said.

The nurse hooked me up to an intravenous line with a cooling water solution, and immediately I began to feel better.

Later that evening, some of our friends visited and prayed for me at the clinic. Gail's prayer partner contacted another friend John to pray for me.

While I lay on the gurney, Gail said, "John received some pictures when he prayed for you. He saw Jesus touch you on the forehead. Then you appeared inside of Jesus' chest. Stripes ran across His chest. I asked him what it meant, but he didn't know."

"I know what it means," I said. "It's like that verse in 1 Peter 2:24—by His stripes I am healed."

"Oh, that's what the stripes mean. Not only that, Jesus carried you!"

All the test results came back negative. The doctor diagnosed the problem as severe dehydration brought on by the fever. Six hours later, I was released.

When we came home, billowing smoke from the kitchen greeted us with an awful burning odor. The soup had simmered all night long. The stainless steel pot had become charcoal black inside with rice kernels looking like chocolate jimmies. Thank God the house didn't burn down!

Yeow! That was some hot soup.

What a wonderful God we have—he is the Father of our Lord Jesus Christ, the source of every mercy, and the one who so wonderfully comforts and strengthens us in our hardships and trials (2 Corinthians 1:3–4 TLB)

~ Bob Kaku

Chapter 6   CHOICES

God has given us a free will to choose life or death—heaven or hell. He wants us to choose life and to choose His Son, Jesus. Every day we can let Him into our decisions and involve Him in our lives.

ôð ᗩᕤ ᕫᖇ

The Bead Shop

Why, oh why, did I do what I did?

My mother enrolled my sister and me in a cooking class when we were teenagers. Every week I disappeared from class, ambled down a steep hill, and headed over to a bead shop.

The store workers cordially greeted me. "Here's how you make this new piece of jewelry," a worker said. "Slide the bead through the headpin. Loop and wrap it around through the jump ring . . ." They taught me how to construct striking jewelry that included cameo rings, earrings, floral-beaded bracelets with matching necklaces, and all types of attractive accessories.

When nobody was looking, I grabbed a few of the sparkly little jewelry beads from my shopping tray and dropped them into my purse. Clink, clink. *That was easy.*

Instead of feeling grateful to the store owner and workers for their instruction, I did the unthinkable. *They won't notice a few missing beads.* Two hours later, I returned to the cooking class, just in time to sample the foods.

Soon stealing from this store became a habit.

I wore the new jewelry to school. By the end of each week, my high school classmates bought practically everything I wore, sometimes fighting over the individual pieces.

A few years later, I found Jesus, and my life began to change. One day when I was reading the Bible, my eyes fell on a verse that struck a chord.

"If he gives back what he took in pledge for a loan, returns what he has stolen, follows the decrees that give life, and does no evil, he will surely live; he will not die" (Ezekiel 33:15 NIV).

My mind flashed back to the bead shop. *Why did I steal from them? What was I thinking?* To rectify the situation, I wrote a letter to the bead shop owner expressing my great remorse. I also told him about my newfound faith in Jesus. I wrote a check for the estimated cost of the stolen items, added tax and a few years of interest, and mailed it with the letter. When I took this step of faith, an indescribable peace filled my heart.

About two weeks later, I received a letter from the owner.

Dear Gail,
I was very moved by your letter and newfound faith in God. I fully accept your apologies and check. Thank you so much. I just returned from a vacation to Israel and discovered many people still hold to biblical teachings and values. I want to wish you the best in all your endeavors and new life with God.

"Therefore repent and return, so that your sins may be wiped away, in order that times of refreshing may come from the presence of the Lord" (Acts 3:19)

~ Gail Kaku

అ ౿ ౼

You Don't Need It

*S*trolling through a tree-lined residential neighborhood, my friend Christine and I puffed our cigarettes on the way home from high school. Had my mom known, she would have killed me. She first learned about it decades later when she reviewed this manuscript and went into a tizzy even after all those years.

The way I behaved and dressed resulted from a desire to look grown-up and "cool." I looked very different than my natural self, having bleached my long shiny black hair to amber and wearing a lot of eye makeup.

When I started college, it wasn't about looking sophisticated and "cool" anymore. I smoked to relieve the stresses of school and my teenage life. I had read in the Bible that our bodies are to be a "home of the Holy Spirit."

Just what does that mean? I reflected on the verse and realized that the Holy Spirit came to dwell inside of me when I invited Jesus into my life. That's when a new life began to unfold.

I no longer wanted to smoke, but I didn't know how to stop. Whenever the craving came upon me, I sensed the Lord saying, "Focus on Me—not on the cigarette." When I put that into practice, it worked. The minute I dwelled on the craving, I succumbed.

During the week of my birthday, I came down with strep throat. I asked the Lord, "If You care about me, why am I sick on my birthday?" When I opened the Bible that day, I randomly turned to the birth of Christ in Matthew 1:18. Imagine—of all the places I could have turned, God directed me to Jesus' birthday. I knew He hadn't forgotten mine.

For ten days the illness lingered, and I didn't smoke. I knew my throat would become even more aggravated.

When I recovered, I reached into my purse for a cigarette. Just before lighting up, I heard a small inner voice say, "You've been without a cigarette for ten days. You don't need it." I was taken aback and pondered the words for a while.

A strong craving still clung to me, and I resisted the thought of quitting. Yet, somehow I knew there was a difference between "wanting" and "needing."

After a fierce struggle, I put the cigarette down and chose to quit.

The Lord had a special purpose for my illness, and it was to teach me this lesson. The craving eventually dissipated, and I fully conquered the habit.

Haven't you yet learned that your body is the home of the Holy Spirit God gave you, and that he lives within you? (1 Corinthians 6:19 TLB)

~ Gail Kaku

❧ 𝓨 ❧

You Have the Right to Remain Silent

9 leaned forward against the patrol car as the officer read me the Miranda rights and clasped my wrists in handcuffs. I had never been in trouble with the law before.

Earlier that evening, I went to a company party at an upscale Silicon Valley restaurant. All day long I hadn't eaten anything because of my hectic work schedule, and I was famished. When I arrived, my colleagues greeted me. "Grab yourself a drink, Bob." While mingling with them, I gulped a couple of beers and munched on some savory clams and light appetizers. As the night progressed, I downed cognac, scotch, and some mixed drinks. Around ten o'clock, I left the party to go home.

Just two miles from home, flashing red and blue lights appeared in my rearview mirror as I was driving on the freeway. *Oh, no!* The patrol car eased behind me as I pulled over to the shoulder.

An officer walked over to my open window and hunched over. "Sir, I saw you weaving across the lanes. Have you been drinking tonight?"

"I had a couple of drinks." The truth was I had six or seven.

"Please step out of the car, sir. I'm going to have you perform some sobriety tests. Now, come over here and walk a straight line."

Piece of cake.

"Now, spread your arms wide apart and touch your nose with your index fingers."

I'm doing okay.

"Now, stand on one leg, hold out your arms, and tilt your head backwards." My leg began to wobble, and I nearly lost my balance. I had to put my foot down to catch myself.

Cold steel handcuffs grasped my wrists. *I'm being arrested?*

The officer opened the back door of the patrol car and pushed my head down. I slunk into the backseat with my hands cuffed behind me. As we headed to the county jail, my mind flashed back to the times I had gotten drunk, drove home, and woke up the following morning not remembering how I got home. One time I dozed off on the freeway and awoke a few seconds after missing my exit. I had to admit this had become a pattern.

When we arrived at the county jail, a sheriff's deputy handed me a Breathalyzer. "Here, blow into this," he said. Afterward he took the device and left the room. He returned five minutes later with a little paper readout. "Your blood-alcohol registered 0.11 percent." The threshold for driving under the influence was 0.10 percent back then. The deputy emptied my pockets and confiscated my keys, wallet, and watch. I was photographed and fingerprinted.

I was the first one in the "drunk tank." About fifteen men joined me as the night wore on, creating a cacophony of slurred and coarse words. Some staggered in with bloodshot eyes and were very disoriented. Others were tough, burly characters I didn't want anything to do with. The crowded drunk tank reeked with liquored breath and dank sweat. I grabbed the sleeves of my dark business suit and shrank away from the other men. One intimidating guy monopolized the jail cell phone for hours. Finally, at 3:30 AM, the phone freed, and I called my friend to pick me up. When he arrived, he guffawed. "I knew you'd get into trouble one day."

At the trial, I planned to plead no contest and expected to pay stiff fines. The judge declared people pleading no contest would face jail time, even first-time offenders.

Jail? What am I going to tell my family, friends, and boss?

Later the judge offered an alternative—weekend community service work. *Whew!* Because my blood alcohol was a lot lower than the others, I received one of the lightest sentences— five weekends.

When I left the courtroom, a man wearing a chic suit approached me. "How many days did you get?"

"What?" He repeated the question. *Oh, he's an attorney.* "Ten days," I answered.

"What was your blood-alcohol level?"

"Point eleven percent."

"Is that all? I can get you off. All you have to do is sign a retainer."

"How much is it?"

"Five hundred dollars."

Just as I was about to take him up on his offer, feelings of deep remorse and guilt came over me.

I was a fairly new Christian but somehow knew that the Lord wanted me to change my ways. *I need to take responsibility for my actions and accept the consequences.* I politely declined his offer and shuffled away.

For five weekends I hacked weeds and did miscellaneous carpentry for the county. I paid hefty fines, and the court ordered me to attend a seven-week alcohol rehabilitation class and two Alcoholics Anonymous meetings. On top of that, my insurance premiums skyrocketed.

"Oh, Lord, I really blew it. I could have killed or injured someone. I could have killed or injured myself. Thanks for this lesson and for saving me from myself."

Don't destroy yourself by getting drunk, but let the Spirit fill your life. (Ephesians 5:18 CEV)

~ Bob Kaku

᷾ 𓅭 ᷜ

Apron Strings

9 have often heard that the first year of marriage is difficult—ours was no exception. Adjustments in living habits, meeting each other's needs and expectations, and family obligations were just a few of the challenges.

Shortly after our first anniversary, Gail and I attended a business fellowship banquet. During the prayer time, a soft voice echoed inside me. *Which way is it—your way or Mine?*

My concentration was shattered. I somehow knew that the Lord was speaking to me about my marriage and lack of honesty.

"What's wrong?" Gail asked.

I snapped out of my reverie to muffled voices and the clinking of silverware on china plates.

Before we married, I owned two parcels of real estate—a primary residence and a rental. I led Gail into believing that I had bought everything on my own. I was ashamed to tell her that I borrowed a substantial amount of money from my parents for the down payments.

When we arrived home, I blurted everything out to her. She shot me a scathing look that incinerated my confidence. "Why did you lie to me? You broke our trust!" Rivulets of tears flowed down her cheeks. "You listen to your mom more than to me. It's because you owe your parents so much money!"

During this time, I had difficulty dividing my attention between my wife and my mom who lived nearby. That put me in an awkward spot, because I was taught to respect my parents.

Gail's rebuke blasted me like a double-barreled shotgun. I had no rebuttal. She viewed my inaction as being tied to my mom's apron strings.

Not knowing what else to do, I prayed in utter desperation. "Lord, help! I followed Your prompting and received nothing but grief in return. I could have kept the borrowed money hidden indefinitely. My parents weren't expecting repayment."

In the next few days, Gail's countenance softened. "You must have prayed really hard," she said. "Something unexplainable happened to me last night. All the anger I had toward you lifted, and my love for you renewed. Jesus healed me."

Gail had a significant amount of savings that she accumulated before we married. We used her money to pay back my parents.

I began to balance my family obligations, giving my wife higher priority. When I took that step of faith, the "apron strings" snapped, and I became fully united with my wife.

"This explains why a man leaves his father and mother and is joined to his wife, and the two are united into one." (Matthew 19:5 NLT)

~ Bob Kaku

☙ 𓅂 ❧

A Better Way

*C*hanging motor oil has never been a problem for me—or so I thought.

When Gail's new Acura Integra needed an oil change, I threw on some old clothes and grabbed my toolbox. I eased her car out of the garage and took it for a spin around the neighborhood to warm the engine. After returning, I parked the car in front of our house. I jacked it up and placed the jack stands under its frame and crawled underneath.

I clamped the socket wrench onto the drain plug and loosened it. The oil gushed into the catch pan and drained out. After I retightened the plug, I reached behind the engine block to find the oil filter. *Yeow!* The engine was hot to the touch.

Although I had a fancy filter wrench with a swivel handle, I couldn't get a firm grasp on the filter. I pivoted the handle up and down and every which way but still couldn't get a grip.

"Arrgh!" An hour passed and the sun started to set. *Maybe I should pour the oil back into the engine and take the car to a service station.*

"Oh, no!" Some dust and grass particles blew into the pan. I couldn't pour the contaminated oil back in.

What should I do?

In a fit of desperation, I prayed. "Jesus, I just can't get this filter off. Please help me!" I crawled out from underneath the car and went into the house to get a drink of water. On my way back through the garage, my eyes locked on to an old filter wrench hanging on the tool rack. It was an inexpensive model with a straight handle. I had thought about throwing it away. A quiet, inner voice said, "Use the other wrench."

Nah, that won't work. The handle doesn't even swivel.

The sky began to grow even darker. *Maybe I should give it a try. I have nothing to lose.*

I crawled under the car again and clamped the old wrench onto the filter. To my utter amazement, it loosened immediately.

Was that You, Lord?

Trust in the LORD with all your heart, and lean not on your own understanding; in all your ways acknowledge Him, and He shall direct your paths. (Proverbs 3:5–6 NKJV)

~ Bob Kaku

⮞ 𓅯 ⮜

The Grass Is Greener . . .

*M*y heart trilled at a rapid cadence every time I spoke with an attractive, charming work associate I'll call Scott. He attentively listened to my problems and gave me his time. But there was one problem—we were both married.

Whenever I talked to Bob, I never knew if he listened. He never bothered to remove his stereo headphones or put down the newspaper or even glance my way if he was watching television. I'd constantly ask, "What did I say?" Often, he was clueless.

God repeatedly warned me through Bible verses and messages at church to be faithful in my marriage and to avoid tempting situations. But I couldn't let go. I continued going out to lunch with Scott, even though warning bells rang inside me with undeniable clarity.

The attraction grew into an obsession, and I entertained wrongful desires that allowed this sin to fester. Something could have easily happened.

During this time, I couldn't help but wonder if my callous disobedience desensitized my heart toward God, and caused me to step out of His favor. His blessings and protection were withheld from me. I had a work-related hand injury that required surgery. I lost my job due to software outsourcing. My investments turned sour.

Overwhelming depression engulfed me. "Jesus," I pleaded. "Please forgive me for my willful disobedience. I repent of my wrongful desires, and I recommit my life to You. Help me not to stray from You."

I sought prayer at various ministries. During the prayer times, three people I didn't know told me my marriage was going to get better. Then one day I attended a healing service for my hand. During the powerful prayer, something inexplicable happened. The spiritual bondage that held me captive completely broke off. God set me free. Although my hand didn't heal, God was more concerned about my spiritual life.

Before my hand surgery, a friend prayed for me and heard God speak to his spirit. "Your hand is connected to your heart," he said.

Huh?

Several weeks after my surgery, I understood what the connection meant. My hand surgery was symbolic of a spiritual surgery that my heart needed because it had become hardened toward God. The Lord spoke to me through a verse:

> "I will give them an undivided heart and put a new spirit in them; I will remove from them their heart of stone and give them a heart of flesh. Then they will follow my decrees and be careful to keep my laws." (Ezekiel 11:19–20 NIV).

God sensitized my heart and restored me back to Him. He spoke to me through a Bible commentary. *Focus on your marriage commitment, spouse's good attributes, and communicate with each other.*

I began to apply His principles, and He began to bring our disjointed marriage back together. My love for Bob revived.

In an epiphany, God showed me I wasn't the best listener myself. I was treating God the same way Bob was treating me. "Oh, Jesus, I'm so sorry! Help me to listen and obey You."

For years I wanted to tell Bob, but I didn't want to hurt him and feared what might happen. Then one night I sensed the Holy Spirit telling me to include this story in our book. *I can't do that! I'm a private person! If I can't tell Bob, how can I write this in a book?* After grappling for days, I took a step of faith and spilled everything out to Bob. It surprised me that he took it so well.

Bob expresses the following perspective:

"When Gail told me about Scott, I didn't become angry and wondered why. I quickly figured out the reasons. I had to admit, I was equally guilty whenever I cast furtive looks at the attractive women at work or those who abounded at the shopping malls.

"One might say, 'It's only natural,' or 'It's okay to look, just don't touch.' But I know I'm called to a higher standard and cannot justify these excuses. I constantly have to ask God for help. I remind myself of the time when I courted Gail. I think about what she means to me today. In those tender moments, I realize how much I love her and do not wish to ever leave her.

"What helps me most of all is knowing that my marriage is a three-way covenant with Gail, Jesus and me. If I let her down, I let Jesus down."

A cord of three strands is not quickly torn apart. (Ecclesiastes 4:12)

~ Gail and Bob Kaku

இ ல ல

The Investor

*A*fter my software engineering job moved overseas, I had so much time I didn't know what to do with myself. For the first time, I couldn't find work because many software jobs were lost to foreign outsourcing firms.

I began to explore other professions. A business associate invited me to a real estate and mortgage seminar. I went to the seminar, dragging Bob along. We pulled into the parking lot and noticed shiny, new Mercedes and BMWs occupied many of the best spots.

A former high-tech worker gave the opening pitch. "I acquired four houses within an eighteen-month period, even though I never owned property before. I did so well; I quit my engineering job. You can do it too!"

The speakers that followed shared similar testimonials. A few of them were even unemployed at the time they joined the program. By the end of the presentations, Bob and I were mesmerized.

How did they do it? Where do we sign up?

We sought the Lord for guidance. During prayer, some images drifted through my mind. "I saw a picture of a Chinese New Year parade with a dragon dancing," I said baffled.

"I think that symbolizes great fortune and celebration," Bob said enthusiastically.

But my spirit felt troubled. "I also saw something that looked like a ball with a sheet tightly gathered around it."

"Like a hanged man?" Bob ventured.

"Oh, yeah. That's what it might be! Then I saw a gavel being pounded."

"Hmm—trouble with the law?" he surmised.

"Jesus, are these pictures from You? Please confirm it. We know Satan masquerades himself as an angel of light and counterfeits Your works. Please guide us Jesus."

Later that afternoon, I did a word search on "dragon" using an online Bible Web site. A verse sprang out at me.

The great dragon was hurled down—that ancient serpent called the devil, or Satan, who leads the whole world astray. (Revelation 12:9 NIV)

Those words gave me the heebie-jeebies.

Just before a follow-up meeting, we prayed again. "Whoa! I received more pictures. This time I saw a toe being cut off."

"That probably means we'll become crippled," Bob said in a sullen tone.

"Good point. I also saw a swift, brown horse running with half of its upper body gradually disappearing. Then I saw an umbrella flipped upside down. I think the umbrella means no protective covering since it's upside down."

Bob sighed. "These pictures aren't encouraging but let's check it out one more time to see if the Lord tells us otherwise."

"Okay."

A representative described the training program in more depth. "If you join the program, you'll work under a coach, pursue a real estate license, and recruit people. But you must use our products—our ARMs (Adjustable Rate Mortgages), real estate agents—"

"But we already have our own real estate agent. Also we prefer fixed-rate loans over ARMs," I said.

"No one uses fixed-rate mortgages anymore. ARMs are the future. Remember, I'm the coach. You need to be teachable."

The higher-ups in the organization's hierarchy shared the commissions and fees on every transaction. They said it wasn't a pyramid scheme, but it sure sounded like one.

After the meeting, Bob wore a dour expression. "I know what the picture of the sheet-covered ball means. It's like suffocating in a noose. They control everything."

"They sure do," I muttered. "I bet the swift, brown horse might be symbolic of moving too quickly and losing half the value. If interest rates rise, we can become overleveraged and get into big trouble, plus real estate prices might be at an all-time high."

We didn't like the way the Lord was answering our prayers. After weighing the pros and cons, we heeded the Lord's warnings.

"You know what's interesting?" I asked.

"What?"

"Ever since my job loss, I've been receiving pictures again. Prior to that, I didn't receive any for thirteen years. Perhaps my rapid-fire schedule and job pressures quenched them."

"Maybe God is giving them to you because you're spending more time with Him."

"The flip side is some people think I'm a psychic, which I'm not. I can't call up these pictures at will. They only come when God gives them to me."

Two years later the housing downturn occurred in the Central Valley where we would have purchased homes had we gone with the program. Record rates of delinquency and fore-closures occurred with declining home prices and rising ARM rates.

We are so thankful that God gave us His warnings and saved us from a lot of grief.

If any of you lacks wisdom, he should ask God, who gives generously to all without finding fault, and it will be given to him. But when he asks, he must believe and not doubt (James 1:5–6 NIV)

~ Gail Kaku

⤳ 🕊 ⤶

Unshakable Hope

*W*ith gleaming eyes, our friend Wendy wore an incandescent smile shortly after arriving at our home for dinner. The slim, attractive brunette gushed, "Guess what, Gail?"

"What is it?" I asked.

"My ex-fiancé, Bill, recently returned from Iraq where he served as a captain in the US Army. He found my business Web site and is now calling me nearly every day."

"That's wonderful Wendy!"

Her necklace danced around as she talked with excitement. "Bill was one of the first soldiers sent into combat. He and his men got stranded on a bridge for days, with bombs going off all around them. The bridge shook violently, and they feared for their lives."

I drew in a deep breath and listened with rapt attention.

"As a result of that experience, Bill rededicated his life to Jesus. He's a changed man and has invited me to visit him in Georgia. In just a few weeks, I'll be in Savannah. I can't wait to see him!"

"That's great news!" I said, stirring the zesty jambalaya simmering in the pan.

Maybe he's the right one for her.

Wendy poured her heart out to Bob and me during dinner.

"I married my high school sweetheart after graduating college. In less than one year, the bottom fell out when my husband committed adultery and left to be with his new girlfriend.

"Shortly after the 'death' of my marriage, I received the distressing news about my brother, Roger, who was diagnosed with terminal cancer. He died two days after Thanksgiving, leaving a wife and two small children. Just before my brother's death, my dad became ill and almost died.

"As if all this grief and trauma weren't enough, I couldn't make the house payments by myself. I was forced to move out of my brand new home into a small one-bedroom apartment. I had no other choice but to rent out my beautiful home, which I later discovered the tenants trashed. My world was imploding.

"In the midst of my darkest valley, I went to Trinity Church in San Antonio, Texas and found Jesus. A peace that surpassed all understanding filled my heart.

"Two years later, I met Bill when I was preparing for graduate school. We got engaged, but soon I discovered we were spiritually incompatible. He had no interest in reading or studying the Bible. He constantly complained about going to church. He rarely prayed or spoke about God. Although Bill believed in Jesus, I knew believing wasn't enough. Even the demons believe and shudder. In short, he was a weak and noncommittal Christian.

"I broke off the engagement, even though I was still very much in love with him."

Twelve years later, Wendy hadn't met anyone she liked as much as Bill, but at the same time, she wanted a man who would lead her in loving God.

After we finished dinner, we gathered in the living room. Sunlight filtered through the plantation shutters and reflected off Wendy's jewelry, making her countenance even brighter.

Bob and I prayed for the Lord's guidance on her renewed relationship.

A few weeks after she resumed contact with Bill, Wendy sought prayer at our fellowship meeting for her relationship with him. During the prayer, I was taken aback when four images skittered through my mind.

I nudged Wendy. "When we prayed for you, I saw a bouquet of long-stemmed pink roses."

She burst out in exuberance. "Bill used to give me all types of bouquets, including long-stemmed pink roses."

"He did? I also saw an old-fashioned wooden carriage with horses."

She effervesced. "He's making arrangements for us to ride a horse-drawn wooden carriage!"

"He is?" I remained silent about the next two troubling images—an old-fashioned toilet with swirling water and then a modern toilet with swirling water.

Two weeks later Wendy flew to Savannah. He took her sightseeing all over in this romantic city, known as the belle of the sultry Southern coast. She had a great time, and he invited her back. A few weeks later Wendy flew back to Savannah but something was missing.

Nothing had changed with Bill. In fact, he had grown even weaker in his faith. Now, he didn't want to go to church at all or talk about God.

Crestfallen, Wendy prayed most of the way home on her flight back to California. A couple of days later, she called Bill and told him she needed to bow out of the relationship. It ended a second time.

Now the pictures of the toilets made sense. The old-fashioned one symbolized her past relationship from twelve years ago, and the modern one, her recent breakup. I decided to tell Wendy.

Her gaze sank toward the floor. "How interesting!"

"Wendy, don't despair. God has other plans for you. Remember that time at Malcolm's party when we prayed? I saw you wearing a velvet crown with a gold trim. Then I saw something that looked like a wedding ring set, followed by other separate rings. I didn't understand why I saw so many rings."

She smiled and rebounded. "Those pictures give me hope that God's best is in my future. I used to wear rings on both hands, but I made a deliberate decision not to wear any rings after my divorce, so a potential mate wouldn't become confused about my marital status. Some guy thought I was married because I wore a ruby ring on my right-hand ring finger!"

We burst into laughter.

"I think it's so neat that you receive pictures," Wendy said with a scintillating smile.

"You receive them too!"

"Yeah, I guess I do."

"God started giving me pictures when I became born again. I think they occur when I spend a lot of time reading and studying the Bible. I set a goal this year to read three chapters a day, along with the notes in a study Bible. Sometimes I listen to an audio Bible. If I do eight chapters a day, I can finish the entire Bible in five months."

"That quick?"

"Yeah. Do the math."

I admire Wendy for not compromising and for waiting upon God to bring the right man into her life.

"Call to Me and I will answer you, and I will tell you great and mighty things, which you do not know." (Jeremiah 33:3)

~ Gail Kaku

Chapter 7   THE LORD HEALS

Jesus came to heal people and restore them to God. Sometimes a healing is immediate and visually observable. Other times a healing occurs over a period of time. Finally there are times when a healing doesn't occur for reasons beyond our understanding. In any event, God is faithful.

ə ὃ̃ ⍺

Right Before My Eyes

9've always been skeptical of miracle healing services. *Are they staged or pronounced in a way such that anyone could feel healed?* One night my thinking changed forever.

A guest speaker shared his riveting, inspirational story at a businessmen's fellowship dinner inside a hotel banquet room and offered to pray for people afterward.

Gail and I sought prayer to break out of a spiritual rut. A teenage boy hobbled on crutches directly ahead of us in the prayer line. Heavy gauze bandages wrapped around his right foot. Soon it was his turn for prayer.

The speaker addressed the boy with great compassion. "What happened to you?" he asked.

"I was in a car accident a couple of years ago. My foot never healed properly."

"Before I pray for you, I need to know if you know the Lord."

"No," the boy replied.

"Do you want to know Jesus in a personal way?"

"Sure."

The boy recited a prayer with the speaker and invited Jesus into his life.

The speaker unwrapped the gauze bandages from the injured foot. Gail winced and quickly looked away from the unsightly foot that was bluish-purple and swollen like a football. He placed his hands upon the boy's foot and prayed for the Lord's healing. *This I gotta see.*

I stood no more than three feet away and had a clear view. I stood quietly observing and waited in anticipation. In the next few minutes, the swelling began to subside. Not only that, the foot began to change from bluish-purple to a normal flesh tone. I stared saucer-eyed with my mouth agape.

The speaker asked the Lord to level the foot that dangled inches from the floor. As he was praying, the heel lowered a notch, then dropped some more. A few moments after that, it touched the floor. By the time he finished praying, the foot looked completely normal.

"Try walking without your crutches," the speaker said.

Without hesitation, the boy set the crutches down and strolled around the banquet room beaming.

I no longer doubted God's miraculous healing power.

They will lay hands on the sick, and they will recover. (Mark 16:18)

~ Bob Kaku

⊰ 🕊 ⊱

I Believe

*M*om held the unmatched record of perfect attendance for ten consecutive years at the insurance company she worked for. No one else came close. But all that changed when she noticed a spot of bleeding and mentioned it to her doctor during a routine physical.

Her doctor conducted a pelvic exam and ran a series of tests. A few days later, Mom received a call. "You have a grapefruit-sized cyst in your abdomen," her doctor said. "You have uterine cancer."

"Cancer?" B-but . . . I feel fine."

"You won't necessarily feel pain. Your condition is serious and will require surgery. My first opening isn't for several weeks. Schedule an appointment."

When Mom broke the chilling news to the family, her words dropped like a bombshell.

My sister Pauline jumped to her feet. "Why can't the doctor operate right away?" She called the doctor and tightened her grip on the phone. "The doctor has a planned vacation," she said, hanging up the phone. Pauline wasted no time and called Cousin Eugene, who knew some good oncologists at the Beverly Hills Cedar-Sinai Medical Center.

Through Eugene's connections, Mom transferred there and saw a team of recommended doctors right away. They scheduled the surgery for the following day.

Mom tenaciously kept her faith and fought for her life. "I'm too young to die. Jesus heal me!" She had the love and prayer support of her family and church friends. She claimed God's healing promises over her life.

Following the surgery, the family met with the oncologist. "Your mom is a very fortunate lady," he said. "We found early stages of ovarian cancer, not the uterine cancer she was diagnosed with. Ovarian cancer is very dangerous and fast spreading. Any delays could have killed her."

A group of doctors consulted together and recommended eight months of chemotherapy. Once a month, Mom went in for chemotherapy from five AM until nine PM. On the nights I picked her up, she looked ashen and listless. It hurt me to see her so weak.

Following the chemo, another surgeon conducted an exploratory operation to assess her condition. He emerged from the operating room with a refreshing smile. "I have some good news for you. All traces of cancer are gone!" We let out a buoyant cheer.

God provided the right place, the right time, and the right doctors.

Today, over twenty years later, Mom is cancer-free and has a special ministry that involves visiting the sick, taking them food, and praying for them.

O LORD my God, I cried to You for help, and You healed me. (Psalm 30:2)

~ Gail Kaku

$$\approx \gamma \ll$$

I Can Breathe

*A*nother sleepless night passed as I coughed up a storm and struggled to breathe. After three days of suffering like this, I checked myself into the emergency clinic.

The doctor listened to my breathing through a stethoscope. "You have bronchial asthma," he said.

"Asthma? I thought that only affects children."

"It isn't unusual to develop asthma later in life. Unfortunately, there isn't much you can do for it except move to the desert."

"Desert?" I grimaced.

"The warmer weather will help your condition. An inhaler might relieve some of your discomfort. Do you want to try it?"

I nodded. He handed me a prescription.

About that time, my company just finished building a new facility in the Southern California desert. A program manager from another department offered me a promotion to a management position there.

Yikes—is the Lord leading me to the desert? The offer flattered me, but I wanted a different type of job. Also I didn't want to live far away from my family and friends. I politely declined the offer.

I continued suffering from severe congestion and coughing convulsions in the nights that followed. The inhaler gave no relief at all. *Did I make the right decision?* I sought prayer for healing at my fellowship group, but nothing happened.

During this time the Lord had warned me to let go of a dating relationship with someone I'll call Jeremy. He didn't know Jesus in a personal way, and his lack of faith dragged me down spiritually.

When I went to a retreat in Seattle, I was sitting under a redwood tree reading my Bible, and a verse leaped out at me:

"Do not be bound together with unbelievers" (2 Corinthians 6:14).

The words shot through me like a bolt of lightning. But I couldn't let go—Jeremy made me happy. After the retreat, I sent him a postcard when I traveled to Western Canada. After mailing it, I lost my expensive gold rope necklace.

Back in California, I attended a church seminar on cults. During the workshop, the pastor all of a sudden changed subjects and bellowed, "Do not be yoked together with unbelievers!" I jumped when I heard it.

Despite the warning, I went skiing with Jeremy at Mammoth Mountain a few weeks later. A reckless skier hurtled off a ridge doing a helicopter spin and crashed on top of me. I lay on the snow unconscious for several minutes. When I got up, I saw stars everywhere. I never had a skiing accident before. To make matters worse, my Nikon camera inside my fanny pack got crushed.

Several days later, my friend who didn't know anything about Jeremy admonished me.

"Don't be partnered with a non-Christian," he said. Yet I went out to dinner with Jeremy that weekend. The following week, my plans for a ski trip to Mt. Bachelor, Oregon went awry. I was caught driving in a blinding snowstorm and could have easily died.

I couldn't help but wonder if my willful disobedience opened the door to Satan, who comes "to steal and kill and destroy" (John 10:10).

I jostled with the thought of giving up Jeremy. I didn't want to let go, but I knew what the Lord was telling me. After reflecting on all the mishaps, I came to my senses and prayed.

"Jesus, I'm truly sorry for rebelling against You and for taking things into my own hands. I rededicate my life to You, and I release Jeremy." My eyes grew hot with tears, and the dam broke.

That evening something mind-boggling happened. Every trace of bronchial asthma I had suffered from for the past eight months completely vanished. I slept soundly through the night without coughing once.

Whoo hoo! I could breathe again!

"See, I am setting before you today a blessing and a curse—the blessing if you obey the commands of the LORD your God that I am giving you today; the curse if you disobey the commands of the LORD your God" (Deuteronomy 11:26–28 NIV)

~ Gail Kaku

Master's Touch

*T*he software code melded together, and my eyes began to glaze over after a long workday. I blinked hard and glanced at the clock—2:10 AM. Since I was no longer productive, I threw on my blazer, grabbed my briefcase, and prepared to leave.

I hauled a large box of computer printouts from the lab to my car. I lifted the heavy box into the trunk and heard a little snap. An acute, shooting pain seared my spine as I stood immobilized. I cried out, "JESUS, HELP!"

A few minutes later, I gingerly eased myself into the car and drove home.

The following day my colleague carried the heavy box from my car into the office. He set it down alongside of my desk. "You didn't know there's a right way to lift a heavy box?" I nodded. He spent the next few minutes demonstrating the proper techniques; flexing his legs and maintaining a straight back.

"Wish I'd known sooner!" For months the pain prevented me from standing or sitting for long periods.

I reflected on a story Dr. Yonggi Cho told when he visited our church as a guest speaker.

"A woman with throat cancer approached me to pray for her healing," Dr. Cho said. "She kept coming back, and every time I prayed nothing happened. Then one day an idea came to me. 'Write your favorite healing verse ten thousand times,' I said to her. 'Come back after you finish your homework, and I'll pray for you again.'

"For weeks the woman diligently wrote and meditated on the healing verse. When she completed the assignment, she came back for prayer. Before I had a chance to pray, she announced, 'My throat no longer hurts.'

"Subsequently she went to see her physician who ran a series of tests. The results showed all traces of throat cancer had miraculously vanished. Then it dawned on her that the healing occurred sometime during her homework. The words she wrote over and over again began to sink into her heart. That's when her faith began to build, and she believed for her healing. This woman standing next to me is the one who was healed."

Dr. Cho lifted her hand up. The audience burst into loud cheers, whoops and applause.

This story inspired me to meditate on a healing verse:

He Himself bore our sins in His body on the cross, so that we might die to sin and live to righteousness; for by His wounds you were healed. (1 Peter 2:24)

I didn't write the verse out but pondered it over and over again.

"Jesus," I cried, "please show me how this verse applies to my healing. Is this a promise I can claim? Is there a command I need to obey? What are You saying to me through this verse?"

I inserted my name into the verse and visualized Jesus dying on the cross exclusively for me. He not only bore my sins, but also my back pain.

For almost a year, I held onto the healing verse. Then one day I bent over to pick something up. I flexed my lower back muscles in different positions without any trouble. All my back pain had vanished and never returned.

Jesus healed me!

"Do not let this Book of the Law [Bible] depart from your mouth; meditate on it day and night, so that you may be careful to do everything written in it. Then you will be prosperous and successful." (Joshua 1:8 NIV)

~ Gail Kaku

❧ 🕊 ❧

Song of Worship

*O*ne Sunday morning, I awoke feverish and whispered to Bob in a raspy voice, "I'm not feeling well. My throat hurts. I won't be going to church."

"Do you want some hot tea, aspirin, or anything?"

"No, maybe later." I shut my eyes and curled up in bed. He readied himself to go without me.

I tossed and turned, unable to sleep. I distinctly heard a faint song resonate in my head.

> *Come let us worship and bow down: let us kneel before the Lord our maker . . .*

I flipped over on my side, buried my head in the pillow, but I couldn't block out the song. I shifted to another position trying to catch some sleep. The song kept repeating. Suddenly it dawned on me. *Maybe God wants me to worship Him in church. Since I can't sleep anyway, I might as well go.*

The moment I rose from bed, I began to feel better. I quickly got dressed and rushed into the kitchen just before Bob left. "I'm going with you after all."

"You are? Are you sure you're okay?"

"For some unknown reason, I feel better now."

While we were driving on the freeway, I turned toward Bob and said, "I don't know why, but I kept hearing the song *Come Let Us Worship and Bow Down.*"

He shrugged.

We entered through the double doors of the sanctuary a little late. The worship team was already singing.

Bob's mouth formed a full-moon circle, and he stared at me round-eyed. "That's the song you heard this morning! Our church never sings that song."

After the song was over, the worship team leader announced, "One more time."

"This church never sings the same song twice," Bob said in stunned amazement.

Jesus, You were calling me to worship You in church this morning!

That afternoon I no longer had any trace of the sore throat.

Worship the LORD your God, and his blessing will be on your food and water. I will take away sickness from among you (Exodus 23:25 NIV)

~ Gail Kaku

ॐ ༀ ॐ

The Needle

$\mathcal{M}$y coworker hovered over me, anxiously awaiting a report I volunteered to program. We weren't scheduled to work on this luminous, blue-sky Saturday, but we had no other time to do it. Both of us were in a hurry to finish and salvage some part of our plans for the day. I was already late for a Monterey bike trip. I rapidly rolled my hand back and forth with the computer mouse when my right hand twisted. Searing pain jolted through my wrist. "Ow!"

The company nurse filed a worker's compensation report and referred me to the company doctor.

"Where is the source of your pain?" the doctor asked. I placed my thumb over the tender spot and described the injury. "That's the ulnar side where your tendons pass through. You have tendonitis." He handed me a referral for two months of physical therapy.

Aren't you going to take any tests?

The therapy made the pain worse. At times, I couldn't even lift a fork. The physical therapist referred me back to the doctor. I returned to the doctor's office and requested an MRI. The company doctor offered cortisone shots instead. I grimaced and declined.

On my follow-up visit, the doctor insisted on cortisone shots again. "It will take care of all your pain," he said.

"Okay, I'll try it this time." He marked the tender spot with a felt pen. While sitting on the exam table, I placed my left hand under my right elbow to hold my hand upright. He jabbed the syringe into my wrist, and my hand jolted. Tears rolled down my cheeks. He yanked the syringe from my wrist and noticed he missed the marked area. He injected me a second time. The needle jab caused me to jump, and he missed again. He shot me a third time. I left his office writhing in pain.

The shots gave no relief at all. In fact, it made my pain worse. I decided to switch doctors and see an orthopedist.

The orthopedist took an X-ray, but nothing showed in the film. On my second visit, he ordered an MRI and bone scan. He carefully examined the MRI slides against the lit panel. "You have a ganglion cyst deep within your wrist underneath a bone. It's a thick gel-like blister," he explained. "There's good news. Your hand can be corrected with surgery and become fully functional again. I'm going to refer you to a hand surgeon, Dr. Gordon Brody."

I did some research and discovered that Dr. Brody was one of the official doctors of the San Francisco Giants baseball team and the 49ers football team, and he specialized in complicated hand surgeries.

Dr. Brody reviewed the MRI slides and confirmed surgery on my hand would be very successful. I breathed a big sigh of relief.

Before I scheduled the surgery, I called the insurance company and was shell-shocked when they denied coverage. They referred me back to the company doctor.

The company doctor cordially greeted me and was surprised to see the MRI slides. He didn't know I had switched doctors. He examined the film in another room and came back five minutes later. "Surgery won't help you," he said.

"But two other doctors said surgery would be very successful."

"That isn't so. Leave the slides overnight so I can review them further."

I didn't feel comfortable and refused. Exasperated, I pleaded, "I need this surgery!"

"I really want to help you," he said, "but the only way you're going to get help is by filing a lawsuit."

My personal insurance wouldn't cover the surgery because of the pending worker's compensation claim. Finally, I closed the claim. Since Dr. Brody was outside of my insurance network, I found a new hand surgeon under my plan. I asked my new doctor her thoughts about the surgery.

"Your hand will never be the same with surgery," she said. "It'll take about a year or longer to recover."

My heart sank. "Have you had a case like mine before?"

"I've never worked on an internal cyst, only external ones. I'd have to make a large incision and fold the skin all the way back."

I swallowed hard. "Is this surgery risky?"

"It's a high-risk operation. A lot of things can go wrong. Your hand will really hurt for about eight weeks."

"Can we try draining the cyst?"

"Sure. We can do it now if you'd like."

I nodded. She set my hand steady on a table and inserted a syringe into my wrist. She pulled the plunger back slowly, but no gel came out. It hurt terribly. I left her office disheartened.

Not knowing what else to do, I sought prayer at my church. A picture of a needle going into my wrist appeared in my mind's eye during prayer. Two weeks later a woman at a fellowship meeting prayed for my hand. She too saw a picture of a needle, then saw a cyst shrinking.

"What does it mean?" I asked. She didn't know. This woman had no prior knowledge of my cyst, the attempted drainage or the possible surgery. *Maybe the Lord wants me to try drainage again.* I cringed.

I went back to see Dr. Brody. "Can we try draining the cyst?" I asked.

"Drainage would be a waste of my time. The cyst is too difficult to get to. I recommend surgery."

"Is this a risky operation?"

"Low risk," he answered confidently.

I looked at him surprised. "How much downtime will I have?"

"About three weeks." His answers gave me hope, and I scheduled the surgery.

Following the surgery, I asked Dr. Brody, "How did you remove the cyst?"

"I cauterized it with a needlelike tool, Bovie Electro-cautery Apparatus. It sends an electrical current through a needle tip that cauterizes the affected area."

I gasped. *That's what the pictures of the needle meant!*

My hand is now back to normal. I thank Dr. Brody who performed the surgery, and I thank God for ultimately healing my hand.

"I will instruct you and teach you in the way which you should go; I will counsel you with My eye upon you." (Psalm 32:8)

~ Gail Kaku

Chapter 8 THE LORD PROVIDES

God wants to meet all our needs and be our provider. This doesn't mean our prayers necessarily get answered the way we want them to. When we ask for things that aren't good for us, He says no, or sometimes He'll allow us to learn from our mistakes. He wants to give us His blessings according to His plan and timetable.

ॐ ✝ ॐ

It Doesn't Make Sense

*F*or years I had a difficult time managing my finances. I ran up my credit cards, paid portions of my bills, and incurred hefty interest and penalties when my payments were late. When I ran out of money, I borrowed from my parents.

After I became a Christian, I heard a teaching about tithing. "The *tithe* is 10 percent of one's gross income," the speaker explained.

Wow, that's a lot of money! I can't afford that.

Later that afternoon I was relaxing at home lying on a lounge chair in the backyard patio. I reflected on the message and became convinced that I needed to trust God with my finances. *Okay, Lord, help me to trust You in this area.*

The following Sunday, my whole body tensed as I wrote the check for the full 10 percent. *Will I be able to pay my bills?* The week after, my fingers struggled to write the tithe check. It was a little easier, but I still worried about having enough money.

I continued to tithe every week. To my utter amazement, I didn't have to cut back on anything. A few months later, I was surprised when I received a promotion and a generous raise at work. For the first time, I actually had money leftover.

When I married Gail, I discovered she not only tithed, but gave offerings to many missionaries, ministries, and to the poor. "Offerings are special gifts above the tithe," she said. "We need to support ministries that spread the Good News of Jesus so people can be saved from their sins."

Now I really won't have any money.

With the extra income Gail brought in, we paid down our mortgage. One year we purchased two new cars with cash. I had never bought a brand-new car without a loan before. Then we bought a rather expensive home in Silicon Valley. Even with the sale of our previous residence, we took out a sizable mortgage. *Now we're going to have to cut back on vacations, dining, and ski trips.* Inexplicably, however, our financial obligations were still being met, and we didn't have to cut back on anything.

Then disaster struck when the economic slowdown hit Silicon Valley. Gail lost her job, and our income plummeted about 40 percent. Immediately, we thought of scaling back on the offering percentage, but later we decided to trust God and left it unchanged. To my utter befuddlement, our financial obligations were still being met. God supplied extra cash through lower mortgage rates, bonuses, and stock options. He provided for all of our needs.

When we give our tithes and offerings, we're giving back a small portion of what God has already given to us. He will provide all that we need.

"But seek first His kingdom and His righteousness, and all these things will be added to you." (Matthew 6:33)

~ Bob Kaku

≈ 🕊 ≈

Trusting God for a Wife

*H*opelessness, wrenching sorrow, and loneliness were just a few of the emotions that jabbed my insides after the breakup with my girlfriend of four years.

"Guess you won't be a Christian anymore," my housemate snickered.

"No, I still am. I made a commitment to God, and there's no turning back."

My girlfriend had introduced me to Jesus, and everyone around me assumed I would revert back to my old ways.

Several months after the breakup, friends and family members began to introduce me to some attractive ladies, but they weren't believers. I knew it would be difficult to share my life with someone who didn't share my faith. I had read in the Bible that a believer should only wed another believer.

"Introduce me to Christians," I told my family and friends.

"We can't help you with that! You're on your own," they replied.

One sleepless night, I kneeled by my bed and prayed from the bottom of my heart. "Jesus, why aren't my relationships working out? Am I ever going to get married? If You want me married, please find me a wife."

Just two months later, I met Gail at a Mount Hermon Christian conference in the Santa Cruz Mountains. We talked for hours about our jobs, skiing, and traveling. *She's not only a strong Christian, but we have so much in common!*

I called her several times a week and racked up the miles driving from Silicon Valley to the Los Angeles area, about 700 miles roundtrip. Everything felt right from the beginning.

Gail was open to relocating, so I promised to distribute her résumé at a Silicon Valley job fair.

I celebrated when she landed a job at a company just seven miles from me. Two months after her move to the Bay Area, I started shopping for an engagement ring. I bought a costly ring, knowing it wasn't refundable. Cold sweat beaded on my forehead. *What if she says no?*

That weekend I took Gail ice-skating and twirled her without having a firm grip on her hand. She went careening on the ice and banged her knee. *Bad move.* She didn't speak to me the rest of the night.

The following evening, I planned to propose. "Gail, let's dress up and go out."

"No, my knee hurts," she snapped. I called a few more times, but she didn't want to talk. Doubts flooded my mind. I tossed and turned all night and prayed really hard.

After three long days, she was feeling better. I took her to a cozy French restaurant that had a Victorian house-like interior. The *maître d'* showed us to a table surrounded by windows draped with lace curtains. Fragrant flowers in a crystal vase and candle lantern sat on top of a mauve tablecloth, creating a romantic ambience. *"Claire De Lune"* by Debussy played softly in the background. I had the opportune time to propose, but the words wouldn't come out. Fear knotted my stomach.

We went back to her townhouse. *Ask her now.* I fumbled for the ring box that got stuck inside my coat pocket. I got it loose, opened the case and took the ring out. Euphoria and terror simultaneously washed over me. "Gail, will you marry me?"

After a pause that seemed interminable, a smile danced across her face. She said, "Yes!"

My heart somersaulted and did a reverse triple flip.

God provided me with a wife after I fully surrendered this area of my life to Him.

Do not be anxious about anything, but in everything, by prayer and petition, with thanksgiving, present your requests to God. (Philippians 4:6 NIV)

~ Bob Kaku

æ ꙮ ᘓ

Trusting God for a Husband

*F*inding Mr. Right is not easy, especially if you're looking for a Christian.

I was vacationing in London and reading my Bible in a
youth hostel when I encountered the verse:

> For the LORD will take delight in you, and your land
> will be married" (Isaiah 62:4 NIV).

I somehow knew God was speaking to me about marriage.
A divine peace descended upon me, and I claimed the verse.

In the years that followed, my dating relationships didn't
work out. Empty affections, wasted intentions, and a broken
heart—I was exhausted. I asked the Lord, "Did you forget
Your promise?"

Then one day, a friend gave me the poem "On His Plan for
your Mate." It conveyed the message that Jesus wanted me to
be fulfilled in an intimate relationship with Him first before He
joined me together with a spouse. The poem brought great
encouragement and hope, and I knew God hadn't forgotten.

I talked to a friend who happened to be a pastor. "I want to
marry a spirit-filled Christian who is a good skier," I said.

Those were just two criteria out of a lengthy checklist. "Will God honor such a request?"

He laughed. "Are you serious?" I nodded. "God will honor the request, but it may take longer."

Sometime later, I went to a conference at Mount Hermon in the Santa Cruz Mountains. The pine scents, chirping birds, and rushing streams made this a refreshing place to draw closer to God. There at the conference I met Bob.

One evening during dessert, he asked, "Gail, have you skied Utah before?"

I looked at him puzzled. "Yes, I have." *How does he know I ski?*

"Where did you ski?" he asked.

"All the majors—Alta, Snowbird, Park City, and Deer Valley." *Oh, I'm wearing my Ski Utah T-shirt.*

"I skied Utah earlier this year."

"You did?" We compared notes and discovered we worked in the same field and had a lot in common. I sank my spoon into my creamy hot fudge sundae. "My job's become old. I'm looking for a change."

"Send me your résumé," he said.

"Ah, sure. Be glad to."

A few days after I returned home to Southern California, I sent Bob my résumé. That same day, I received a letter from him. My pulse quickened as I opened the envelope. Soon he started calling and visiting me. One day he surprised me by sending me a beautiful bouquet of long-stemmed red roses to my workplace.

When my friends visited, I asked them to pray for guidance on my relationship with Bob. During the prayer time, a faint picture of hands and wedding rings appeared in my mind's eye. I gasped. *Jesus, is this from You?*

Bob distributed my résumé at a job fair. He told one company I was coming up to the Bay Area for the Labor Day weekend to visit my sister's family. The recruiter scheduled my interview for the holiday weekend.

After the interview, the manager extended me an amazing offer with a generous raise and relocation allowance, including airfare to look for housing and a professional packer to help with my move.

That weekend Bob visited me at my sister's home and took me sailing in his Lido 14. Cotton candy-like clouds floated across the blue skies. Sprays of water splashed all over us when the boat turned into the wind. He let out the flapping sails when the wind blew from behind, causing the boat to glide across the lake. He pulled the tiller toward him, and the boat changed direction. What a blast!

That evening, he sautéed thin slices of beef, tofu, and fresh vegetables in a sizzling pan and made a delectable Japanese meal called *batayaki. Yum.*

I moved to Silicon Valley a month later. A friend leased two small bedrooms in a townhouse to me at a reasonable price. Every aspect of my move worked out so effortlessly.

Soon after that, Bob proposed. It felt so right. I recalled the picture of the hands and wedding rings and knew this was God's plan for me.

Joy burst inside me like Roman candle fireworks.

After eight long years since that time in London, God fulfilled His promise to me.

Now to Him who is able to do far more abundantly beyond all that we ask or think (Ephesians 3:20)

~ Gail Kaku

ॐ ᚚ ᚘ

Make an Offer

I gawked at the mailer in total disbelief and made a beeline into the house. "The transportation authorities want to put the BART train in our backyard!" I bellowed.

Gail jolted from her desk chair and reached for the mailer. "They wha-at?"

We had just given our house an extensive makeover, adding new carpets, fresh paint, two bathroom remodels, and a cosmetic facelift to the kitchen. We even made the landscaping look different, removing a colossal palm tree and yucca trees from the front and back yards.

Two alternate routes were being considered for the Bay Area Rapid Transit (BART) extension from Fremont to San Jose. The constant whir of electric engines and beeping of horns would disrupt our peaceful neighborhood.

"I'm afraid the mayor and city council favor the more costly, roundabout route that'll run behind our backyard," I said with disdain. "Not only that, they're talking about an elevated track!"

"I don't want a train looming over our backyard. People could look straight down into our home," Gail rasped. "That's an invasion of privacy!"

After collecting ourselves, we prayed. "Lord, should we move? Please guide our decision."

We didn't receive any clear-cut answers and began looking for another house.

We didn't find anything we liked.

Over the years, talk about the extension subsided because of funding problems. We made other improvements to our home that included a new roof, patio, water pipes, and pool equipment.

Our next project was to design our dream kitchen with a granite countertop, light-maple cabinets, recessed lights, and wood floors. We visited a kitchen specialty store and selected a granite stone in an attractive black color with some gray in it. Having a small kitchen proved frustrating and vastly limited our options.

Besides the kitchen, Gail wanted to replace our plush carpet with Berber and redo our tile entryway with marble.

Just as we were about to start the kitchen remodel, the BART talks resumed, triggering the emotional roller coaster all over again. Gail's eyes smoldered like fiery embers. "No, not again! We've been going back and forth on this for eight years now."

"Whether they build the extension or not, let's move," I said. I contacted my friend's real estate agent, and we began looking for a suitable house.

Gail prayed. "Jesus, please guide us to a brand-new house that is bright and airy with large closets. And close to our jobs—"

"Dream on. We can't afford that!"

A few days later, I stumbled across a listing on a real estate Web site for a brand-new, contemporary-style house close to our jobs. The price was high, but not beyond reason. I called our real estate agent and arranged to see it during my lunch break. Gail already had lunch plans and couldn't make it.

My agent and I walked up the paving-stone driveway and stepped into the house. Sunlight streamed through the large front window, brightening the living room with a radiant glow. The light maple floors and high ceilings created a light and airy ambience. I ventured into the kitchen, and my eyes widened in astonishment. *This is the kind of kitchen Gail wants.*

We ascended the Berber-carpeted staircase and toured the bedrooms. *Didn't Gail want Berber?*

When I explored the master bathroom, I was surprised to see a deep, oversized Jacuzzi tub enclosed with attractive marble tile. *Wow! This is far better than the Japanese soaking tub I've been wanting.*

I reached for my cell phone and called Gail. "This house has everything you've been wanting and more. The kitchen even has a black granite countertop similar to the stone we picked for our remodel."

"It does?"

"And the kitchen has light maple cabinets, wood floors, and recessed lights—"

"Really? I can't believe it has all that."

"But there's one problem. The house is in an old neighborhood."

"That doesn't bother me. Make an offer," she said.

I held off until she had a chance to see it later that night.

Gail toured the house with a luminous smile. "I really like this house! I know how the Lord works, and it's an answer to my prayers."

The agent claimed she had another offer that was more than the asking price. In the red-hot real estate market, bidding wars were common.

We looked at each other in dismay. "Lord, if You want us to have this home, make it possible," Gail prayed.

We adjusted our offer and hoped for the best. Later that day, we rejoiced when it was accepted.

After signing the sales agreement and exhaustive paper-work, our real estate agent said, "Homes in your old neigh-borhood aren't selling fast."

"They aren't?" I said with concern. *With the BART issue, it might be even more difficult.* We had to sell our house to be able to afford the new one.

As we were leaving the real estate office, Gail had one of her bright ideas. "Let's go to church tonight to hear the guest speaker, Tim Storey."

I was dog-tired and not enthusiastic about going, but went anyway.

Tim declared in his opening statement, "Some of you will be able to sell your home, while others have difficulty."

My mouth dropped wide open. I turned toward Gail and asked, "Why is he talking about real estate?"

She gave me a knowing smile. "I don't know about you, but I came to church to receive a word from God, and that word is for me. We're going to be among those who sell quickly."

We had one open house and received fourteen offers. The first two fell through, but the third one materialized.

Delight yourself in the LORD; and He will give you the desires of your heart. (Psalm 37:4)

~ Bob Kaku

෨ ᗵ ഛ

God Save Our Bathroom!

*7*wo years after we moved into our newly constructed home, we noticed hairline cracks forming in the tiles of our master bathroom—all over the floor, shower walls, bath skirt, and even on top of the vanity counter. It looked like someone took a piece of chalk and drew lines on the tiles. The longest crack measured four feet and ran across multiple tiles. Where did these cracks come from?

"Lord, help! What's happening to our bathroom?" Gail wailed.

I called the builder, and he came over to examine the problem. He squatted down toward the bath skirt and ran his finger over the crevices. "I think the problem is in the marble," he said with a puzzled expression. "I'll get back to you." But we never heard back from him.

"It looks like we're stuck since we didn't extend the home warranty," Gail lamented. "Who would have ever thought a new house would have such problems!"

Two bathroom contractors came over to assess the damage. "This job will be very difficult due to the size of your tub," the first contractor said. "There's nowhere to move it. If it breaks, we won't be able to get another one up the stairs and through the doors. We'll need a crane to pass it through the window."

I peered through the window and looked down at the small gap between our house and the neighbor's. "But there isn't any room for a crane."

The second contractor measured the length of the bathroom and reached for his camera. "I've never seen anything like this before." He furrowed his eyebrows in bewilderment. "I think it's an installation problem. Or maybe it's the foundation."

"Foundation? The builder thinks it's the marble," Gail interjected.

"Why isn't the builder repairing the bathroom? He can fix it a lot cheaper since he's already familiar with it."

"He doesn't return our calls," I replied.

"That's too bad. Most builders carry insurance to cover these types of problems. I think California has a law with a provision called *Latent Defect* that protects consumers from hidden problems in new construction. You may want to look into it. My brother is a lawyer who specializes in these types of cases. I'll give you his number."

I'd hate to file a lawsuit.

A few weeks later, repair quotes came in at roughly $25,000. "Wow! How are we going to pay for this?" Gail asked.

"Let's file a claim with our insurance company."

The insurance company sent a structural engineer to analyze the problem. After several weeks, he concluded the probable causes were either material or workmanship which the insurance didn't cover.

"What are we going to do?" Gail looked at me with concern. "Let's contact the builder again."

He refused to discuss the bathroom repair and insisted we go through our attorney.

"Lord, we don't have the slightest idea of what to do next. Please guide us!" we pleaded.

A few days later, something compelled Gail to call our realtor. She came over to examine the cracks and suggested we file a complaint with the State of California Contractors' License Board. Not knowing what else to do, we followed her advice.

A woman from the board called within a week. "I have eighty complaints ahead of you," she said. "I don't know when I'll get to your case."

The news discouraged us. A week passed, then two, followed by a third. The woman from the board called again. "Did the builder contact you?"

"No," I answered with curiosity.

"You still haven't heard from him? He could lose his contractor's license."

"Is that so?"

The following day, I almost dropped the phone when the builder called. He came over to see us and presented us with a proposal. "I'll pay half," he offered.

"Why should we have to pay for any of it?" I countered. We held our position, and the builder backed down. He agreed to take care of the full repair.

After seven months of wrangling, negotiating, and praying, our bathroom was fixed.

"You never know how God is going to answer prayer," I chuckled.

But those who hope in the LORD will renew their strength. They will soar on wings like eagles; they will run and not grow weary, they will walk and not be faint. (Isaiah 40:31 NIV)

~ Bob Kaku

Chapter 9 ROYAL FAMILY

Jesus is the King of kings. When we receive Him as our Lord and Savior, we're adopted into the Royal Family. A new life of meaning, purpose, and adventure awaits us as we seek Him and develop our relationship with Him.

~ ✣ ~

The Chaperone

*O*ne spring day, when I was wrapping up my freshman year of college, my younger cousin Amy called. "Hey, Cous', can you do me a big favor?"

"What is it, Amy?"

"My high school girl's club needs a chaperone. Twelve of us have been going to Newport Beach every summer since grade school. We stay at a really nice beachfront home for a week. Can you be the chaperone? I know how much you love the beach. All your expenses will be covered."

My face lit up. "I'd love to, but I've never chaperoned before."

"Doesn't matter. I need this favor. Please, oh please—"

"What do I do?"

"Nothing. Just be there. The parents just need someone older than us, and you're eighteen."

"Are you sure it's okay?"

"Of course."

"Sure, I'll do it."

I was older all right, but in many ways Amy and I were more like peers. I'll never forget the time we yanked the screen off the front window of her bedroom and jumped out while the neighborhood boys waited for us. When we returned a few hours later, my aunt caught us red-handed crawling back in. *Uh-oh...*

Those were my high school days when I spent a couple of weeks every year at Amy's home and had the time of my life.

A few days before leaving, I mentioned the trip to some of my college friends. "I'm a bit nervous since I've never chaperoned before."

"You'll do fine. We'll come visit you," they said.

If I have any problems, my friends will bail me out.

While I was driving to Newport Beach with Amy, I sought the Lord with all my heart. "Jesus, please help me with the chaperoning. I don't know what I'm getting myself into, but I place it into your hands." Just moments after that, a peace beyond understanding filled my heart.

Shortly after we arrived, Amy, her two classmates, Vivian and Sharon, and I strolled down to the beach. We sat on our beach towels and basked under the golden sun. We watched the cobalt-blue surf crash upon the sand and create white foamy bubbles. Vivian started singing worship songs. Amy and I chimed in.

"The songs are so beautiful," Sharon said with her sky-blue eyes gleaming. She didn't know any of the songs.

I turned toward her and said, "We're singing worship songs because we're Christians."

Vivian explained to Sharon, "God loves us so much that He sent His Son, Jesus, who sacrificed His life to free us from our sins. When we make Jesus the Lord of our lives, He forgives our sins and gives us eternal life in heaven. He offers us a new and abundant life far greater than anything we can imagine. Do you want to receive Jesus into your heart?"

"Yes, I'd love to!" Sharon replied with a cheery smile. With childlike faith, she invited Jesus into her heart through a simple prayer. Tears of radiant joy spilled over the attractive blonde's face. We celebrated her new birth in Christ with exuberance.

By midweek, trouble brewed. The dishwasher overflowed, splattering suds all over the kitchen floor.

Then some guy on the beach sexually harassed Lisa from our group.

On top of this, another girl took off with her boyfriend and didn't return that night.

Where are my friends when I need them?

If that wasn't enough, the doorbell rang and one of the girls bellowed, "Gail—the police are here. They want to talk to you."

Police? My heart began to drum at a rapid pace as I hurried to the doorway.

"Are you the chaperone?" an officer asked. I nodded. "Two of your girls were out after curfew."

"There's a curfew?"

"Yes, a beach curfew is enforced nightly at ten PM."

One of my girls offered the police officers some cheese puffs and soda.

"No thanks," they said to her.

"I'm sorry. I was not aware of the curfew," I said.

"We just arrested some other people a couple of blocks away."

"You did?" A bolt of fear shot through me and jangled my nerves.

The officer's expression softened. "I'll give you a warning this time, but if your girls are caught a second time, they'll be arrested. Be sure it doesn't happen again."

"Thanks for the warning," I said and shut the door.

The girl who had taken off with her boyfriend returned two days later, worried that she might be pregnant. *Where are my friends who promised to help me?*

When I read the Bible that day, certain words jumped out

at me, "Destroy the idols that you've made." The same words resounded in my mind a few moments later. Then a third time.

What idols?

Then it dawned on me that an idol can be anything we reverence more than God. Jesus wanted me to bring my problems to Him first, rather than rely on my friends.

Okay, Lord, please help me with all these problems!

On another day, Vivian engaged in an intense discussion with Holly and Debbie about the rise and fall of the anti-Christ, the rapture, and Jesus' second coming.

Amy and I joined the discussion. After several hours, they wanted to receive Jesus into their lives. During the prayer, Debbie squealed, "I see Jesus standing in the flame of the candle! He's wearing a white robe."

We opened our eyes and turned our heads toward the lit candle perched on the coffee table. At that moment, the flame fizzled out. No one had blown on it, nor were the windows opened.

God must have given Debbie a personal vision to confirm her faith. I was ecstatic. Initially, three of us were Christians, but now, the number had doubled.

As the week progressed, more and more girls became interested in Christianity. The new converts sparkled with joy and talked about their faith with other classmates. Several more girls received Jesus.

Vivian and I prayed with the girl who was worried about being pregnant. To my surprise, she also received Jesus and began to trust Him for a new life. Several weeks later the girl found out that she wasn't pregnant after all.

Every morning we awoke to the gentle sounds of the ocean waves. We reveled in the most spectacular sunrises and sunsets that painted the sky with a myriad of rich colors—yellow, gold, scarlet, fuchsia, and purple—changing by the minute. Even more beautiful were the lives of those who met Jesus.

By the end of the week, eleven of the twelve girls were Christians.

Through this experience, God taught me to rely on Him first. After I let Him in, the problems worked themselves out, and these wonderful salvations occurred.

On the last day of the beach trip, some friends arrived mid-morning and stayed several hours. Shortly after they left, another group of friends showed up. After they left, more friends arrived at night and stayed until the wee hours. God put my friends back into my life after I learned to bring my problems to Him first.

This turned out to be such a blissful week that is forever etched into my memory.

And there on the beach we knelt to pray. (Acts 21:5 NIV)

~ Gail Kaku

Friends

*E*very weekend I got together with my friends from college to play tennis. Some evenings, we waited hours for a lit court. Whether we played or not, we had a blast telling stories and laughing on the courts. We always grabbed a bite to eat afterward and talked into the wee hours. None of them were believers.

"Lord, how do I reach out to my friends? I've tried talking to a few of them about You, but they didn't seem open. I so desire that my friends spend eternity in heaven rather than in the lake of fire. I give You this tremendous burden, and I claim each person's salvation."

One day when I was reading the Bible, the following verse jumped out at me:

"The smallest one will become a clan, and the least one a mighty nation. I, the LORD, will hasten it in its time" (Isaiah 60:22).

I sensed the Lord saying He would draw my friends to Himself. It would start small, but grow and multiply. An inexpressible joy flooded my heart, and I claimed God's promise.

I invited my friend George to church after telling him how I found God. After he heard about my winnings on the radio contest, he prayed, "God, if You want me in church, fix my stereo for me." He shuffled over to his broken stereo, pressed the ON button, and the music sounded. His eyes and mouth grew round. Soon George started coming to church and joined the youth group led by a dynamic leader. I was ecstatic when he received Jesus into his life.

Today, George says: "I believe the Lord has a special plan for everyone. Often, it isn't what you want, but what you need. Everyone in my family is a committed Christian. My son loves to read the Bible. My wife and I are instilling biblical values into the kids, so they can pass it on to future generations."

Another tennis friend David laughed skittishly when I invited him to church. "I'll see you in church on Sunday," he said. But he never showed. A few days later, we ran into each other on campus. "I'm really coming to church this week."

"I don't believe a word you say!"

A few weeks passed and David called. "You know, Gail, when you said you don't believe a word I say, it really bruised my ego. I can't have you think of me that way. I'm a very responsible person. Your words bothered me so much that I finally came. It wasn't easy. I'll be in church again next week."

After several months, David received Jesus into his life.

Arlene came shortly after with her atheist boyfriend. I almost fell off the pew when Arlene, a former Buddhist, gave her life to the Lord.

Ross scowled when I invited him. "No way! This isn't for me!" One day, after many months, Ross shocked everyone and came to church. Since then, he has become strong in his faith.

Today, Ross says: "Becoming a Christian has helped me to prioritize my life and focus on maintaining a stable family; rather than making the highest salary, living in the nicest home or driving the ultimate car. We're all active in church, and my kids know Jesus. There's a lot of pressure in my job. People play all types of political games to make their numbers, but I'm convicted to do what is right even if it costs me my job. It's important to me that I don't compromise or do anything unethical in the workplace. God gives me His strength and sees me through the difficult times."

"Why are all my friends going to church?" Karen wondered. She decided to check things out for herself and soon joined us.

Joyce, Tim, Steve, Brian, Doug, and others started coming. *Wow! We're becoming a clan, Lord.* I held on to His promise, "The smallest one will become a clan, and the least one a mighty nation."

The friends I invited to church invited their friends, and those friends invited other people. Soon people outside the tennis group started to come. Many gave their lives to Jesus.

Today, God is still fulfilling His Word by multiplying this clan through the group of tennis buddies and their families and friends.

"Not by might nor by power, but by My Spirit," says the LORD of hosts. (Zechariah 4:6)

~ Gail Kaku

Love Scrolls

*M*argo, a loving, effervescent, and dear friend from our fellowship group wrote all the names of her unsaved loved ones on a piece of paper and rolled it up like a scroll. She then tied a ribbon around it and placed it into a basket. "Jesus, please guide each of these loved ones to your priceless gift of eternal life in heaven. Don't let anyone die in their sins," she pleaded. She read every name written in it.

What a great idea! For years Bob and I tried reaching out to our loved ones, inviting them to church, outreach programs, and other events. Nothing worked. Several times, I'd wake up in the middle of the night trembling for all those precious people who weren't saved.

Hearing about the scroll gave us hope. We created our own with blue-rice paper and rolled them up with gold ribbon ties.

"Jesus, we present You with our scrolls. We bring every person before You, not only the ones on the scrolls, but people of all nations. Your Word in 1 John 5:19 says that the whole world lies in the power of the evil one. Set the people free from Satan's strongholds. Open their eyes before it's too late. Let them find You. Send the right person across their path who will point them to You, so they can experience Your deep love and rich blessings. Most of all, guide them to Your gift of salvation so they can spend eternity in heaven."

Our hearts thrilled when my nieces, Kelly, eight, and Trina, five, attended a weeklong children's camp sponsored by our church, Jubilee Christian Center.

"Camp was so much fun, Auntie Gail! I want to go back again next year," Kelly said with light in her eyes.

They spent the weekend at our home. Kelly plunged off the diving board and glided across our backyard pool like an Olympian. When she surfaced for air, she gushed, "Auntie Gail, I received Jesus into my heart at camp."

I nearly dropped the lemonade I was holding. "You did, Kelly? I'm so happy for you!" Trina remained quiet as she swam in the shallow end.

A few weeks later, they came over for swimming again. While Kelly was treading water, she announced, "Trina also gave her heart to Jesus at camp."

"She did?" I stared in wide-eyed wonder. "Congratulations, Trina!" A winsome smile appeared on her face as she floated across the pool.

"Trina sings worship songs in the shower," Kelly said.

"She does?" I smiled.

A few years after that, Bob and I were elated when his niece Sarah, seven, and nephew Brian, four, accepted our invitation to the Christmas party at our church. Brian shuffled to center stage, dancing and celebrating Jesus' birthday with the other kids, wearing a birthday hat, and blowing a whistle. "Your church is so much fun," Sarah said. "Brian and I want to come back!" The following week, we picked them up for children's church and continued doing so for the next five years.

Then one Sunday, Sarah said with a lilt, "I accepted Jesus into my heart at church today."

Joy bubbled up inside me. "That's wonderful, Sarah! I'm so happy for you."

We moved out of the area, and Sarah and Brian stopped going to church. We were greatly disappointed.

Then one afternoon when we were at a family gathering, Sarah said to us, "I saw you walking across the church parking lot today."

Bob and I looked at her baffled. She was now a teenager in high school and a recent homecoming princess.

"I've been going to Jubilee with my boyfriend for a year now."

"You have? We're so glad you're back in church!" Bob said with a half-moon grin.

Today, these children have become young adults and talk about their faith.

Kelly, a recent graduate of Illinois College of Optometry says: "I'm so thankful that Jesus gives me hope when, at times, everything seems so bleak. My life has meaning and purpose, now that I live for Jesus. He is the only constant in this ever changing world. I'm so glad He's my closest friend and personal savior."

Trina, a student at Cal Poly says: "Ever since I received Jesus into my life, I have a passion to serve needy people and those who aren't saved. Now, I'm not so selfish and independent anymore. I try my best to treat everyone with respect, even though I feel some people don't deserve it. It's my desire to follow Jesus all the days of my life."

Sarah, a student at Hawaii Pacific University says: "Jesus made a significant impact on my life ever since I got saved. He's embedded inside of me and affects my decisions in every aspect of my life. I thank Him for His unconditional love, mercy, and gift of salvation."

Brian just started UC Santa Cruz, and says: "Jesus is an integral part of my life and gives me His strength to carry on even when things are tough. I praise my Creator for all things."

We lifted our scrolls up toward heaven and prayed, "Jesus, please continue to draw every family member, relative, friend, neighbor, and people of all nations to You! It's unthinkable if one person were to perish."

"Believe in the Lord Jesus, and you will be saved—you and your household." (Acts 16:31)

~ Gail Kaku

෨ 🕊 ෨

Shout!

*I*t was one of those days. I tried everything and nothing worked.

Whenever we visit Gail's mom in Southern California, I try to make myself useful by doing some home maintenance. She knows I'm not very handy and gives me only the easy tasks.

This time, the water filter cartridge needed replacing. I shut off the water valve under the kitchen sink and removed the filter housing. I tried to twist the filter cap off, but it wouldn't budge. I used my upper body to wring the cap open, but *nada*. Then I tried to force it open with a screwdriver, but it still wouldn't loosen.

Gail walked into the kitchen and saw me struggling. "Let's pray," she said. "Jesus, we know You want to be involved in even the little things. Please help Bob with the water filter."

After she prayed, I reached for the cartridge and tried the cap again. "It still doesn't come off."

"Why don't you see Dave?" she suggested.

He was a professional contractor who had originally installed the water filter system. I strode to his house a few doors away and rang the doorbell. Nobody answered.

Shuffling back to the house, I thought about calling the manufacturer. I dialed the 800 number listed in the owner's manual and a recorded message played. "Technical support is not available. Please call back next week."

They're closed? It's not a holiday.

Gail stepped into the kitchen and heard me grunting. "Stop! You'll break it!" She pulled the screwdriver away from me and set it on the counter. "Okay, we tried prayer. We tried Dave. We tried technical support. What else is left?" She tossed her hands in the air. "Oh, I've got an idea. Let's try a shout."

"Huh?"

"You know how the Lord calls us to do spiritual warfare."

"You mean like the Hebrews did before battle?"

"Exactly. Let's try a victory shout."

"You do it. What would the neighbors think?"

"No, you need to do it too. It's not enough to only hear God's Words. You need to apply it. Remember someone from our prayer group said you've become complacent? You know God hates it when we're lukewarm. You need to rise up and fight. Be an overcomer."

"All right," I replied reluctantly. We shuffled to the living room, and Gail led a shout at the top of her lungs. I shouted but with half her volume.

"Let's do it again," she said.

I groaned.

"C'mon honey. You need to return to your first love. You remember what it was like when you first received Jesus. He doesn't want a one-sided relationship. Don't let your fire snuff out."

"All right." The second time, I shouted louder.

"One more time," she said. On the third try, I mustered all my strength and shouted full-throttle. I didn't care what the neighbors thought anymore.

I went back into the kitchen and tried the cap again. This time it twisted right off. I was flummoxed.

When the trumpets sounded, the people shouted, and at the sound of the trumpet, when the people gave a loud shout, the wall collapsed (Joshua 6:20 NIV)

~ Bob Kaku

☞ 🕊 ☜

Abundant Life

"*W*hat is this abundant life that the Bible talks about?" I asked the Lord. "My life's rather humdrum. Aren't we supposed to have joy?"

I gazed at the Bible on the coffee table. "Jesus, the Bible is packed with all kinds of miracles. Why don't they happen today? I'd like to see a string of miracles."

Sometime later, my friend Hiran called. I first met her at a Christian fellowship group in Gardena. *There's something different about her. Why is she so radiant all the time?*

"Gail, can you come over for the weekend? I want you to meet some of my friends and visit my church. It's the neatest place."

"Sure, I'd love to." A recent breakup with my boyfriend left me with more time, plus I needed a break from my college studies and part-time job.

I jotted down directions to Hiran's place and headed over there for the weekend. About six of her friends greeted me. As the evening progressed, I noticed something remarkable about each of them. Their eyes sparkled with overflowing joy. By contrast, my life was devoid of joy, and I suffered from low self-esteem and self-condemnation.

"Let's pray," Hiran said. Moments after that, the stereo blasted in the apartment above us, vibrating the room we were in. One gal in our group declared, "I rebuke that music in the name of Jesus!" A split-second after that, the music shut off. My jaws dropped.

Hiran's friend Vickie was going through insurmountable financial problems. Another gal in the group began praying for her. Halfway through the prayer, she paused. "Vickie, the Lord just showed me that He has a gift for you. Your rent is paid in full. You don't need to sell your car. Just receive it."

Vickie's eyes danced with joy. "Thank You Jesus!" she cried out.

Everyone heard God speaking to them but me. People gave one another an encouraging word or picture from God. *Wow! This is the string of miracles I've been looking for.* I was enthralled.

Then someone asked, "Gail, are you baptized in the Holy Spirit?"

"What's that?"

"It's a gift from God that draws us closer to Him. It's different from water baptism." She opened her Bible and read the following Scripture:

"I baptized you with water; but He [Jesus] will baptize you with the Holy Spirit." (Mark 1:8)

She set her Bible down and elaborated further. "When we are baptized in the Holy Spirit, God gives us power to do His will. Do you want to receive this gift?"

"Sure," I replied without comprehending any of it.

Everyone gathered around me and started praying. After a few minutes, my spirit burst forth with the most exhilarating joy I had ever experienced like a bubbling fountain spilling over. God's overwhelming love enveloped me and gave me a peace I had never experienced before. The low self-esteem and self-condemnation I struggled with earlier completely lifted off. My spirit felt as free as a bird released from a cage. For the first time, I felt deeply loved by God and was swept away with overpowering ecstasy.

The next morning Hiran awoke praising and thanking the Lord. I never heard anyone worship that way before. Later I discovered gratitude and praise is key to receiving joy.

When we arrived at her packed church, I was amazed to see so many beaming and friendly people. I had already come down from the spiritual high of the previous day. When the worship began, the people sang with such great passion. Then one person spoke in tongues and another person interpreted. My eyes grew wide in amazement. Then the pastor read a passage of Scripture, expounded upon it, and delivered a rich and powerful teaching that came alive for me. Not once did my mind drift.

Driving home from Hiran's, I brooded over the setbacks in my life. I also worried about my term papers for school. Halfway home, I asked the Lord, "How is it that Hiran and her friends hear Your voice? Why don't I hear from You in the same way?"

A few seconds passed, and I was astounded to hear God speak to my spirit. "It's because you drown yourself with the radio and focus on your problems. Give Me your undivided attention." I immediately turned the radio off and began to rid myself of distractions. I quieted my heart. Within moments, a thought entered my mind: *Invite your friends Christine and Joyce to church tonight.*

Was that You, Lord? I had invited Christine to church umpteen times before, but she never came, nor had Joyce. It would be a waste of my time to call them.

I hesitated, then called Christine. My eyeballs practically popped out when she said she would come. I called Joyce and her boyfriend answered. "Joyce isn't home." As we were talking, Joyce walked into her apartment. I couldn't believe it when both Christine and Joyce came to the youth group meeting at church that evening. Christine also brought her sister Cindy. I knew God had spoken to me.

Through this experience, I learned Jesus wants to give us special instructions to do His will daily. I learned to pray, "Jesus, what is on Your heart today?"

He has answered me through thoughts and ideas, people, scriptures, songs, impressions, events, circumstances, and in countless other ways.

On another day, I came across the following commentary when I was studying the Bible.

Receiving the full benefits of God's plan for our lives requires us to receive and obey God's commands fully.[1]

God's blessings require full obedience to His commands. "Jesus, thanks for showing me the way to the abundant life."

"Be still, and know that I am God; I will be exalted among the nations, I will be exalted in the earth." (Psalm 46:10 NIV)

~ Gail Kaku

[1] Life Application Bible New international Version Co-published by: Tyndale House publishers, Inc., and Zondervan Publishers House © 1988, 1989, 1990, 1991. All rights reserved. Extracted used by permission, p.629.

Chapter 10   PERSONAL INVITATION

God gives us a choice to live a fulfilling life according to His plans and purposes or go our own way. This is the most important decision you'll ever make and determines where you'll spend eternity.

ই ৺ ৶

Father's Love Letter

AN INTIMATE MESSAGE FROM GOD TO YOU.

The words you are about to experience are true.
They will change your life if you let them.
For they come from the heart of God.
He loves you.
And He is the Father you have been looking for all your life.
This is His love letter to you.

My Child,

You may not know me, but I know everything about you...
Psa. 139:1

I know when you sit down and when you rise up... Psa. 139:2

I am familiar with all your ways... Psa. 139:3

Even the very hairs on your head are numbered... Mat. 10:29-31

For you were made in my image... Gen. 1:27

In me you live and move and have your being... Act 17:28

For you are my offspring.... Act 17:28

I knew you even before you were conceived... Jer. 1:4-5

I chose you when I planned creation... Eph. 1:11-12

You were not a mistake, for all your days are written in my book... Psa. 139:15-16

I determined the exact time of your birth and where you would live... Act. 17:26

You are fearfully and wonderfully made... Psa. 139:14

I knit you together in your mother's womb... Psa. 139:13

And brought you forth on the day you were born... Psa. 71:6

I have been misrepresented by those who don't know me... Jno. 8:41-44

I am not distant and angry, but am the complete expression of love... I Jno. 4:16

And it is my desire to lavish my love on you simply because you are my child, and I am your father... 1 Jno 3:1

I offer you more than your earthly parents ever could... Mat. 7:11

For I am the perfect father/mother... Mat. 5:48

Every good gift that you receive comes from my hand... Jas. 1:17

For I am your provider and I meet all your needs... Mat 6:31-33

My plan for your future has always been filled with hope... Jer. 29:11

Because I love you with an everlasting love... Jer. 31:3

My thoughts toward you are countless as the sand on the seashore... Psa. 139:17-18

And I rejoice over you with singing... Zep. 3:17

I will never stop doing good to you... Jer. 32:40

For you are my treasured possession... Exd. 19:5

I desire to establish you with all my heart and all my soul... Jer. 32:41

And I want to show you great and marvelous things... Jer. 33:3

If you seek me with all your heart, you will find me... Deu. 4:29

Delight in me, and I will give you the desires of your heart... Psa. 37:4

For it is I who gave you those desires... Phi. 2:13

I am able to do more for you than you could possibly imagine... Eph. 3:20

For I am your greatest encourager... 2 Ths. 2:16-17

I am also the Father/Mother who comforts you in all your troubles... 2 Cor. 1:3-4

When you are brokenhearted, I am close to you... Psa. 34:18

As a shepherd carries a lamb, I have carried you close to my heart... Isa. 40:11

One day I will wipe away every tear from your eyes and will take away all the pain you have suffered on this earth.... Rev. 21:3-4

I am your Father, and I love you even as I love my son, Jesus... Jno. 17:23

For in Jesus, my love for you is revealed... Jno.17:26

He is the exact representation of my being... Heb.1:3

He came to demonstrate that I am for you, not against you... Rom. 8:31

And to tell you that I am not counting your sins... 2 Cor. 5:18-19

Jesus died so that I could be reconciled... 2 Cor. 5:18-19

His death was the ultimate expression of my love for you... I Jno. 4:10

I gave up everything I loved that I might gain your love... Rom. 8:38-39

Come home, and I'll throw the biggest party heaven has ever seen... Luk. 15:7

I have always been your Parent, and will always be your Parent... Eph. 3:14-15

My question is ... Will you be my child? Jno. 1:12-13

I am waiting for you ... Luk. 15:11-32

Love, Your Dad. Almighty God

~ Barry Adams

❮ ✣ ❯

RSVP

*D*o you see popcorn miracles in your life? We believe that everybody has them. But many people think of them as mere coincidences, serendipities, and the like.

When you know God in a personal way, you'll begin to see His hand in every part of your life. He wants to have a vital, communicative relationship with you and be your best friend.

We all have wrongs in our lives known as sins that hinder our relationships with God because He is perfect and holy. The only way we can have this barrier removed is to put our full trust in Jesus Christ and receive Him as our Lord and Savior. He paid the penalty for our sins by dying on the cross.

> "For the wages of sin is death, but the free gift of God
> is eternal life in Christ Jesus our Lord." (Romans 6:23)

It's not enough to be a "good" person—we all need the new life God offers us through Jesus and His incredible gift of salvation. This miracle is the ultimate miracle.

God made you to last forever. Your physical body will die one day, but your soul lives forever.

The afterlife is real and more permanent than your present life, whether you choose heaven or hell. God wants to spend eternity with you in heaven; but He gives you a choice.

Come and join the Royal Family. Jesus is the King of kings who wants to crown you and adopt you as His child. He loves you so much and has an awesome plan that only you can fulfill through Him. God the Father; His Son, Jesus; and the Holy Spirit are one God, known as the Trinity.

You can receive Jesus into your life and begin your personal relationship with Him by applying the following:

Acknowledge: We have all sinned and fallen short of God's glory. (see Romans 3:23)

Believe: God loves you and sent His Son Jesus to die for your sins. (see John 3:16)

Confess: Jesus rose from the dead and lives today. (see Romans 10:9)

Apply your faith and recite this prayer:

Dear Jesus, please help me to turn from my sins and live my life for You. I invite You to come into my heart. Forgive me for all my sins. Please guide every area of my life and be my King, my Lord and personal Savior. I believe You are the Son of God. You died, then rose from the dead for my salvation. Baptize me in the Holy Spirit. From this day forth, I live by faith in a growing relationship with you. In Jesus' name, Amen.

If you prayed this prayer for the first time, visit the Popcorn Miracles Web site at: www.popcornmiracles.com and click on WELCOME.

When you begin to walk with Jesus and talk to Him, you will learn to recognize His voice and a new life of meaning, purpose, and adventure unfolds as we seek Him and develop our relationship with Him.

All those wonderful miracles that happen day after day— things you once called coincidences—will now be precious gifts from your Heavenly Father to you. You'll not only spend your life thanking and praising Him for giving them to you, but most of all, you'll praise Jesus for being your closest and most intimate friend.

"Salvation is found in no one else, for there is no other name under heaven given to men by which we must be saved." (Acts 4:12 NIV)

May you experience a life of Popcorn Miracles!

~ Bob and Gail Kaku

ABOUT THE AUTHORS

Bob Kaku has been a Christian for over 20 years. He works as an information technology manager at a health care company. Gail Kaku has been a Christian for 30 years. Her background is also in information technology. They live in the Silicon Valley area of California.

Printed in the United States
123274LV00002B/516/P

9 780979 990304